D1137663

'*Feeding Johnny* is a must-read for a business owners. It tells the warts-a~~~ ~~~ ~~~~~~, ~~ ~~, and former colleague, Colm O'Brien, as he learned his craft, made a career and built his business. There are business and life lessons peppered through *Feeding Johnny*, told with humour and compassion. I loved it!'

—Bobby Kerr, dragon from RTÉ's *Dragons' Den*, chairman of Insomnia Coffee Company

'*Feeding Johnny* is well worth reading if you are thinking of starting a business or perhaps have just started one. It contains very practical advice gained from experience in the School of Hard Knocks. Colm tells how to overcome the numerous difficulties/ obstacles that come your way. I am happy to recommend *Feeding Johnny*.'

—Patrick Bewley, Bewley's Coffee Company

'*Feeding Johnny* is an inspiring story from an inspirational man. It takes a look into the bright and dark sides of being a business owner. The honesty with which Colm recounts his experience is refreshing and makes for compelling reading. He offers many fantastic insights into the habits and skills that got him to where he is today. Whether you're looking to start out in business, or you are a seasoned entrepreneur, there is plenty of learning to take from this book. Intertwined amongst the many marvellous stories are some real nuggets, which can be applied in both business and everyday life.'

—John McNamara, Evolve Life Coaching

'*Feeding Johnny* is a book I couldn't put down. Not only is it one of the most inspirational business books I have read but, in sharing his personal journey as an entrepreneur, Colm gives both the aspiring and current entrepreneur so much to think about and so many tips and strategies that can be implemented with immediate effect.'

—Dave Sheahan, founder of Dreams to Reality

'[*Feeding Johnny*] is a well-written and very entertaining biography of [Colm O'Brien's] entrepreneurial journey. I am sure it will provide an inspiring example to others looking to start their own business.'

—Jim Clemmer, leadership author and
workshop/retreat leader, Canada

'Colm O'Brien has written an awesome book here. I really enjoyed reading it. It is a real life story and has the good, the bad and the ugly moments peppered throughout with good old fashioned Irish humour. What I liked most about this book was the simple home truths Colm gently reminds us about. If you are looking for a book to uplift your spirits and at the same time give you hard evidence of what it takes to defy the odds and overcome massive business challenges to ultimately succeed then look no further than *Feeding Johnny*.'

—Steven McGeown, performance coach, London

Feeding Johnny

How to Build a Business Despite the Roadblocks

Colm O'Brien

First published in 2015 by
Liberties Press
140 Terenure Road North | Terenure | Dublin 6W
T: +353 (1) 405 5701| www.libertiespress.com | E: info@libertiespress.com

Trade enquiries to Gill & Macmillan Distribution
Hume Avenue | Park West | Dublin 12
T: +353 (1) 500 9534 | F: +353 (1) 500 9595 | E: sales@gillmacmillan.ie

Distributed in the United Kingdom by
Turnaround Publisher Services
Unit 3 | Olympia Trading Estate | Coburg Road | London N22 6TZ
T: +44 (0) 20 8829 3000 | E: orders@turnaround-uk.com

Distributed in the United States by
International Publishers Marketing
22841 Quicksilver Dr | Dulles, VA 20166
T: +1 (703) 661-1586 | F: +1 (703) 661-1547 | E:
ipmmail@presswarehouse.com

ISBN: 978-1-909718-56-2
2 4 6 8 10 9 7 5 3 1

A CIP record for this title is available from the British Library.

Internal design by Liberties Press
Cover design by Liberties Press
Cover image Justin Farrelly/*Sunday Times*, edited by Simon Dry

Contents

This book is dedicated to Aideen, known to her close friends as Aido, my wife, who, despite knowing all there is to know about me, chooses to be my life partner.

Thanks Aido

Love ya x

Acknowledgements

This book would have remained on my bucket list, undone, without the assistance of a handful of key people.

Pat Slattery, my long-time friend, rang me in late 2012 to say that his partner, bestselling author Donna Kennedy, was running a one-day seminar entitled 'How to Write a Bestseller in Twenty-one Days'. I was turning fifty in 2013, so I decided to treat myself to her course. I owe you Pat.

Donna Kennedy was superb! She cut through the myths about writing a book and, in a few short hours, pointed me and the others in the room in a direction that each of us was comfortable with. Her 'system' is what gave me the confidence to try; my sticking to her system is what allowed me finish. Cheers Donna.

Mark Lloyd, another long-time friend from Limerick, offered to become my 'line editor' and stuck with me for months as I fumbled and stumbled through the process. Without Mark, *Feeding Johnny* would have been all but unreadable. His patient, professional eye and diplomatic guidance helped me get the manuscript into a shape that allowed Liberties Press take a look and make a considered decision to back it. Thanks Mark.

Finally, I thank Sean, Sam and Karen in Liberties Press for having the courage to publish *Feeding Johnny*.

And you, dear reader, I thank you for picking it up. If you want to get in touch with feedback or would like to discuss your own business journey, mail me at feedingjohnny@carambola.ie.

Introduction

This book is about you.

I'll tell my story but, make no mistake, this book is really about you. Whether or not you choose to put pen to paper in the future, I believe you are writing your own story one day at a time on the pages of history. I know that, as you explore this book, you'll find insights that will help you take the next step in your personal journey.

So let's begin.

My name is Colm O'Brien and I'm a Dub happily living in Limerick with my better half, Aideen. We have three wonderful children: Shóna, Steven and Jenna. And we own a business. It trades as Carambola Kidz – Healthy School Lunches Delivered. In this book, you will read about our successes and failures as we have navigated the stormy, uncertain waters of a post-boom economy.

Several years ago, I was invited to talk to a group of students in a Start Your Own Business (SYOB) programme. Bernadette Farrell, founder of Ace Training, had invited me in to tell my story. It seemed to go well – I certainly enjoyed it – and I was invited back. Now, whenever Ace Training is contracted by an Enterprise Board to deliver a SYOB programme, I get wheeled out for an hour to tell it as I see it, warts and all.

The wonderful thing about this story is that it is being written while I am still in the trenches. Every day, I get up and do my best to move my business forward – much like the SYOB participants.

Each year, my story has moved on, so it is always fresh. However, in meeting hundreds of SYOB participants over the past several years, I have been staggered to realise a couple of home truths:

- Almost none of them read business or personal-development books.

- Very few of them understand the difference between being self-employed and owning a business! (I can sense a few eyebrows rising already!)

I believe a problem for those who are considering starting businesses, or have recently started businesses or are struggling with their businesses, is that books offering business lessons are usually:

1. Books written by theorists – people who have studied how to start, build and grow businesses, but have never done it themselves. The value of this type of book is questionable. You can only learn to swim by getting into the water. If you have never been in the water, how can you write a book purporting to teach me how to swim?

2. Books written by the mega-successful (many of whom I admire, by the way), who have it all together. These entrepreneurs own multi-million-dollar – even multi-billion-dollar – global organisations that straddle continents and are, despite their stories of overcoming, in the envious position of having 'ploughed their fields'. Most people I meet that are starting out can't see themselves achieving at that level and, I fear, might be put off by such books.

This book is different. I have started, built and grown businesses, but I'm not quite at the billion-dollar level yet.

What I'd like to do is invite you to journey with me as I struggle with building my business, and ask that you allow me to travel with you (through my musings) as you progress. Deal? OK.

One more thing before we get started. I want to make it easy for you to *finish* his book, so let me propose this plan for getting you to the end.

I organised this 185-page book into eight chapters with ten sections each. In reading, as in anything, consistency is the key, so I want to introduce you to my Ten-a-Day Programme: read for ten minutes a day or read ten pages each weekday, whichever you can manage. If you do the former, you'll finish in about two months. If you do the latter, which I recommend, you'll finish within a month

Use your body clock to the max here. If you are a morning person, like me, do your ten a day first thing. If you're a night person, like my wife, do your ten a day last thing at night.

Let me congratulate you on taking the next step in your journey. Enjoy!

CHAPTER 1
Carambola Kidz Today

What Does Carambola Kidz Do?

Let me tell you where Carambola Kidz is as a business today, and then we will get into the real story – the events, the people, the coincidences and the possible Divine interventions – that allowed us arrive here.

We make packed lunches. Healthy packed lunches for primary-school children. More than twenty thousand of them every day. And here's the kicker: each one is different!

Yep, we make twenty thousand individually tailored packed lunches for twenty thousand unique children. Each lunch bag has a child's name, class, teacher, school, personally chosen menu – which can be different every day – and calorie count. We deliver them all around the country before 10.30 AM every school day! Easy-peezy, lemon-squeezy. Well, not quite.

Do you have kids? Do you know someone with two or three primary-school kids? Do you know what it takes to make two or three lunches every day? They don't want this and they don't like that and you've run out of bread and the ham has curled in the fridge. Multiply that by a few thousand, and you begin to get the picture.

So, each school day, the wonderful Carambola Kidz team mobilises to produce twenty thousand fresh, individually chosen lunch bags and then delivers them all around the country, *before* 10.30 AM!

I *love* Christmas! For me, it is one of those special times of the year and, around Christmas, when schools are closed, I like to reflect on the year just ending and consider the year ahead. I'm an

early riser too; a lie in for me is when I get up at perhaps 7.30 AM. So, at Christmas, one of my favourite habits is to get up in the dark of the early morning and sneak downstairs. I make coffee: fresh, *never* instant – a legacy of my Bewley's days. Then I turn off all the lights except the ones on the Christmas tree, and I just sit. Magic.

This Christmas just gone it struck me that, despite some difficulties in our business which I'll tell you about later, we had reached a very important milestone. We had supplied our *16 millionth* healthy packed lunch in December. And we still had *never* missed a delivery.

Yep, our 16 millionth. Huge!

Did I see this coming when we started out? No way. We just started. We took the first step and that led to a second and a third and a three hundred fifty-fourth, and – well, you know where this is going. Each day, we simply took more steps in our journey.

For those of you interested in the numbers:

- Started: October 2003

- 2014 turnover: €5 million

- Lunches produced: more than 16 million

- Accuracy Level: 99.999984 percent

- Delivery record: 100 percent

- Jobs: more than 150 directly and indirectly employed

- Premises: five – Limerick (HQ), Dublin, Wexford, Westmeath and Galway

So that's what we do. And we are blessed. And we are grateful for the opportunity.

Heeere's 'Johnny'!

It was 5 AM on a dark, cold November morning in the wilds of Mayo. Rimas, our north-west driver, was on his third cup of luke-warm coffee from his flask when suddenly . . . nothing. The engine had died! Rimas was engulfed in a perfect, dreadful quiet – apart from the sound of the wind howling outside. The cab was warm, but Rimas and the hundreds of healthy packed lunches in the refrigerated section in the back of the van were stranded. It wasn't Rimas's fault that the van had broken down but what to do now? He rang people, he woke people up and the Carambola team got behind him. Within an hour, his still-dead van was on the back of a low-loader repair truck. And where did he ask the low-loader to take him? To every school on his route so he could *feed Johnny*!

This is one of the many examples of stuff we have gone through to feed Johnny – a unique one, in fairness, but indicative of the kinds of struggles we face. We've had punctures, crashes, snow, ice, rain, wind, road closures, early mornings and weather warnings to contend with. But Johnny always got fed. We've even arrived at schools in heavy snow, only to find that the local school staff and children hadn't made it! And so we've trudged back to HQ, satisfied that we've done our piece.

Why do we operate to such a standard? Simple, really. We feed kids. We don't have the luxury of saying, 'Well, the weather is bad' – or the truck broke down, or the supplier never delivered – 'so we'll get to you tomorrow, is that OK?' None of that matters. The *only* thing that matters is that we feed Johnny!

So, who is Johnny? And where did he come from?

Johnny Moloney is a made-up character who represents our customer. Johnny is any child anywhere who we have agreed to feed. The super Carambola team I referred to earlier is made up of mums and dads and big brothers and sisters and aunties and uncles and grannies and granddads, all of whom share our passion for feeding Johnny, on time, in full, every time.

I first introduced Johnny to the team during one of my rants about doing the job right. It has always been a belief of mine that the most important thing is to do the job right – because, from that, the money will flow. It's never the other way around. So, somewhere along the line, feeding Johnny became the way we measure how we are doing.

Did we feed Johnny today? Was he fed on time? Did he get what he asked for? Was he happy with the quality of his lunch? Was he happy with the service he received? Were all of our costs in line as we fed him today? Were all of our personnel properly trained and in good form as we fed him? Etc.

Our lives have become very simple. If a problem arises anywhere in our business, the team defaults to a definitive 'feed Johnny first, ask questions later' position. When Rimas's van died, he knew he still had to feed Johnny. So he did.

Meet the Team

'Who speaks English?' was my first question as I met four new, fresh-faced Polish employees in Raheen Business Park one Sunday in 2005.

I had finally managed to find a buyer for all the café furniture I had left over following the failure of my café business earlier in the year. (More about that later – and no skipping forward, by the way.) It was all piled in a store-room in our first production facility. A truck was due any minute to take it off my hands.

So, to clear the store room, I had called in some of the new staff we had recruited.

'Who speaks English?' I asked.

'Me,' said a skinny young man with glasses, timidly.

'OK, you're in charge,' I said, shaking his hand. 'What's your name, by the way?'

'Máirtín,' he replied.

And so we set to work. I showed him what I wanted done and let him get to it with his three countrymen. Within a few hours, the place was cleared. I had an empty storeroom and four new Polish staff members, one of whom seemed to have leadership qualities.

Máirtín turned out to be Marcin (pronounced 'mar-cheen'), and Marcin turned out to be a computer scientist. In fairness, he was a good geek, a conscientious geek, a hardworking geek who had been willing to take a risk in coming to Ireland, a land of opportunity for many Poles at that time.

Marcin found Carambola and, over time, Carambola found a man who has assumed responsibility for all of our IT infrastructure, all of our facilities-management and all of our transport network. Not bad. A good find for both sides.

That is largely how it's been as people have found us, one by one. Many great people – and a few dodgy ones, it has to be said (they know who they are) – have come through the doors. All we do at Carambola is offer opportunity. Those, like Marcin, who saw the opportunities fit their lives, chose to rise and grow with the challenges and are still around. Those who didn't, aren't. It's as simple as that.

For example, Lil, head of accounts – or 'head of making sure there's a few bob in the bank', as we like to say – was our original bread-butterer. She found us when she was ready to re-enter the workforce. Her claim to fame is that she was replaced by two, not just one, buttering machines. Lil's only stipulation when she started was that she didn't want responsibility. Over time, we changed her mind.

Dorota, head of operations, was labelling sandwiches when an opportunity arose to assist us in a trial of our early IT system. She stepped up and never looked back.

Rachel, Carambola's customer care manager and nutritional adviser, was a self-employed trainer, teaching kids about nutrition. She went to a parenting expo with a friend. She shouldn't have been there; she had no kids at the time. I had just been let down by another person, who had promised to do a nutrition-for-kids session in one of our schools. Rachel and I had a coffee. We hired her for a one-day gig. Almost a decade later, she's still here.

I could write about them all, but the others will have to forgive me – maybe next time. People turn up. We allow them in. They choose to perform or not. I love them all.

'Where Did You Get the Name?'

It's one of the questions I'm frequently asked when I speak to SYOB students. It's a good question.

One often thinks that business names are the results of hours of expensive consulting time ploughed into brainstorming, and searching for values associated with particular words, to see if they will suit market dynamics and demographics.

Or perhaps an interesting business name is the invention of some individual creative genius who spits this stuff out in his or her sleep?

Maybe. But that's not how it happened for us. The name Carambola Kidz came about through a series of happy accidents sometimes referred to as 'universal' or 'divine' intervention. It's an interesting story in which my part is so small it's laughable.

First, we need to go back to the failed café.

Our first business was a franchise – a Bewley's Café franchise, to be precise – which opened in 1992 on Cruises Street, a pedestrian area in the heart of Limerick City. We took it over in 1998. It failed in 2005. (Again, no skipping ahead.)

Circa 2000, some business neighbours of ours who ran a small fancy-furnishings store were expanding. The Tiger Cub was growing fast, and Oliver and Caroline Moloney – no relation to Johnny, by the way – were ready to grow. And fast.

They built a twenty-thousand-square-foot furniture emporium called Instore on Ellen Street, close to Cruises Street, and asked whether we would consider putting a coffee shop on the soon-to-be-built mezzanine. 'No problem,' says I – and so we did.

It was a loss-leader for Instore, at least at the beginning. They wanted customers to visit their store, browse and then sit over a €2 cappuccino on the mezzanine, debating whether to spend €1,200 or €1,500 on the lovely sitting-room suite downstairs. It worked beautifully as part of Instore.

But it didn't work for us. So, after six months, we agreed on an exit package and sold the equipment – heavily discounted – to Instore, shook hands (very important) and went our separate ways.

Our adviser, a school friend, Tim O'Keeffe, had had the foresight to insist we operate the Instore café through a limited company. I'd said, 'No problem, Timo, get us one of those.' And he had.

The paperwork we'd received from the Companies Registration Office had basically said, 'You are now the proud owners of The Carambola Ltd (Company number 327466)', a random 'shelf' company, and I'd thought, *That's a funky name*, thrown the documents in a drawer and got on about running my new coffee shop.

So, by the time we passed the reins to the Moloneys we had a company, The Carambola Ltd, with trading losses sitting inside it.

The Importance of a Good Brand

Imagine a white swipe on a black background, and name the brand. You're driving down the road and see a large yellow 'M' in the distance; name the brand. You're in a social setting and see a harp on a pint glass; what drink does it represent?

Brands fascinate me. They are so simple, and yet they can have such deep meanings and associations in the public psyche.

Good branding can enhance a business, bad branding hurts it. Some brands and their trademarks are as valuable as the businesses they represent. Take Coca Cola, for example. It's reported that the business is worth about $96 billion – and that the brand accounts for nearly 20 percent of that value. So we should all consider our branding carefully.

Let me give you an example. Let's say someone from Ballygolacky starts a business. It's an aluminium-windows business, and they call it Ballygolacky Windows. On one level this name seems fine. It tells prospective clients exactly what the company does: windows, not doors, walls, floors, ceilings, swimming pools or coffee. But it also tells clients *where* it does windows: Ballygolacky. So, even if I'm in the market for windows, if I don't live in Ballygolacky, I'm unlikely to call.

The business name has defined the business, but also parochial-ised (limited) it. Clearly, some parochial-sounding brands break the mould, such as Kerry Group, a brand that now spans the globe and uses to its significant advantage global awareness of the reputations of Kerry and Ireland as green lands with tremendously wholesome food heritages. But Ballygolacky Windows? Is it likely to be a global brand? I don't think so.

So when our 'school lunch thingy', as our accountant referred to it, was beginning to grow, he suggested I run it through The Carambola Ltd. And so I did. School Lunch Thingy is up (or down) there with Ballygolacky Windows as business names go – unlikely to inspire. I knew we'd need something better.

One of my favourite brands is the best-known Irish brand in Ireland, next to Guinness: Bewley's. Synonymous with quality coffees, teas, breads and breakfasts – and its iconic spiritual home on Grafton Street in Dublin – Bewley's has been around since 1840. Most Dubliners have frequented Bewley's on Grafton Street; many country people 'up for the day' have enjoyed a breakfast or sticky bun and coffee within its hallowed halls, on the plush red booths under the world-famous Harry Clarke windows. Poets, lovers, film stars, politicians and the homeless have all visited the place (often at the same time), and Sir Bob Geldof penned the Boomtown Rats' hit 'Rat Trap' there in the 1980s.

I am privileged to have carried the Bewley's torch as general manager of Bewley's on Grafton Street from 1991 to 1995 and, in that time, I was instrumental in launching Bewley's Café Theatre, which has itself become an institution. In 1995, I became Bewley's franchise manager and brought the idea that became Bewley's Hotel at Newlands Cross to my then boss, Bobby Kerr, latterly of Insomnia and RTÉ's Dragons' Den fame. Bobby and I brought it to fruition, and it radically changed the Bewley's landscape and the scope of its brand forever.

So when I decided to leave and go into business for myself, I chose to start with a recognised brand behind me, rather than fly my own kite. The brand is bigger than the individual. My first foray into business was a Bewley's Café franchise. I believe in brands.

Carambola Kidz Is Born

So there we were in Limerick, running our very own Bewley's Café franchise and, for reasons I'll explain later, we started our 'school lunch thingy' from the very same premises on Cruises Street. But, by 2003, it was clear the café wasn't going to last, so I went searching for a home for this fledgling new business.

Our butcher, Noel O'Connor, told me of a place in Raheen Food Centre. I rang a contact in Shannon Development who shall remain nameless. He said the alluded-to building was much too big for me. I was majorly ticked off and suggested that, while that may be true, I'd like to see it for myself. So I rang my dad in Dublin. Dad and I went to visit. And do you know what? The Shannon Development guy was right. It *was* too big for us, at that time, but it was *just big enough* to allow us grow. He had seriously misjudged his prospective client.

Most importantly for me, the new space had a room that I could envisage hosting a boardroom table. I could see the opportunity this much-too-big premises held. And so we moved in. And we started to work hard. There were three of us then: me, Limerick native Robert Cribben and a young Polish girl called Bogusia, who had been working in our café. We started packing lunches.

But now we had a problem: overheads. You see, when we operated from the café, all the bills – from rent to electricity to whatever – were the preserve of that business. Now all the costs associated with the new building had to be paid from the sales of school lunches. And so I looked at the next adjacent market, Cork.

Tommy O'Brien – or 'the Da', as he's fondly known by me, my brothers, sisters and 'the Ma' – is the best salesman in Ireland. I, on the other hand, had never sold anything in my life, having spent the previous quarter-century in cafés, where people simply turned up and we gave them what they were looking for. All of a sudden, I was completely outside my comfort zone.

So I rang the Da again. This time, we went to Cork together, and we found a client. We agreed a delivery date two weeks out, so I bought my first Merc. No, not what you're thinking – a fairly rough-looking, second-hand, refrigerated Mercedes Sprinter van for deliveries!

Now that I had my Merc, I thought I'd better sign-write it, to get some value out of driving around, and so I started saying, 'Carambola, Carambola, Carambola Kids, yep that'll work.' I changed the 's' to a 'z' simply because children mess stuff up all the time. Then I decided to Google 'carambola' to see what it would throw up and, to my surprise, I found out that it meant something: a carambola is a star fruit.

Now *this* excited me! Here we had a business, a food business, with a name derived from the star fruit. How cool was that? So I set about creating a trademark for the business, and there was only one thing it could be – a star! I chose a double-gold-star trademark, and I wrote it in black Comic Sans MS letters on a white background. And so Carambola Kidz was born. Ta-dah!

Our Mission

There is an epidemic sweeping the Western world – an obesity epidemic. In Ireland in 2014, almost two-thirds of men and half of women are classified as overweight or obese. Regrettably, children aren't immune; more than one in six boys and one in four girls are either overweight or obese.

Historically, poor meant skinny. Poorer people couldn't afford sufficient food, and so their frames became thinner. In Ireland today, as in other Western societies, poor tends to mean overweight or obese. Why is this? According to Irishhealth.com:

> The US food industry produces far more food than it needs and, therefore, forceful marketing is needed to sell the excess to the American public. At the root of this marketing drive is everyone from farmers to fertiliser manufacturers to restaurants and food companies.
>
> In addition, social changes have affected how we eat. Western society has become a fast-food culture, and the breakdown of family units and family meal times has led to an "on the hoof" approach to food.

These factors may have begun in the US, but they are affecting our lifestyle here in Ireland. We are getting fatter and, unless we do something about it, we are facing some really tough times ahead as a nation, health-wise.

Fast food and heavily-processed foods are readily available and relatively cheap, and they are appealing to our convenience-centric natures. The problem is nutrition – or rather, the lack of it. I have heard it said that we have placed convenience and flavour higher on our list of what's important than nutrition and our long-term health, and I think that's true.

We at Carambola Kidz find ourselves in a space where we can influence children's habits, and we take that as an opportunity to collaborate with those working hard to educate the next generation. We have identified something very simple, but very powerful: if you start a child off in primary school with a healthy diet, you can help them form healthy lifestyle habits. So that's what we attempt to do.

Austrian neurologist, psychiatrist and Holocaust survivor Viktor Frankl has been quoted as saying, 'We detect, rather than invent our missions in life.' And so, resulting from the work that we have done since we started in 2003, our mission has emerged: to promote healthy-lifestyle awareness in all children. (Our original mission was much simpler: to sell school lunches to help pay the rent!)

Rachel Mescall Fitzpatrick, our head of nutrition, works tirelessly with our suppliers to ensure that any product we offer is the best in its class. The litmus test for us is, 'Would we feed our own children this?' If not, it doesn't get on our menu. There are some school-lunch suppliers that say they are just like Carambola only better or more local or whatever, but they offer pizza, sausage rolls, Oreo cookies and juice drinks laden with sugars and additives. Hello?

Meet Cara & Bola

'Who makes your lunches?' I asked eagerly, as a room full of sixth-class girls stared back at me rather apathetically.

Rachel and I were on tour. We were out visiting some of our schools, to make sure that the job we were doing was relevant to them and was working for them. It's something we have done from early on as a company, and there is often nothing better than getting in front of a class full of kids to help validate (or challenge) the work we do. But there's some truth in the old film-making axiom that one should never work with children or animals, because there's no telling what might happen.

So there we were in Cork. Roomful of girls looking at us. Asking questions and getting responses. But to my question 'Who makes your lunches?' the responses were not what we had been hoping to hear; they ranged from shrugged shoulders to 'Is it the caretaker?' They really didn't care. Rachel and I felt like all the work we were doing to provide quality, healthy, nutritious lunches was a waste of time. The children just weren't engaged.

And so it was that, on the drive back to HQ in Limerick, Rachel uttered the immortal words, 'We need characters. We need something for the kids to relate to.' She went on to suggest that they be called Caram and Bola. Around that time, there was a cinema chain in Ireland called UCI. When you went to the UCI, you were treated to cartoon characters called 'U-C' and 'I', so what Rachel had suggested had a precedent, but it felt unwieldy. So I thought about it for a while.

Enter Simon Dry of Dry Design. Simon was a graphic designer I had met first when he was contracted to work with Bewley's.

He added the diamond shape along with the coffee beans behind that brand, a design that remained unchanged for almost two decades. He also created the pink-and-purple logo on your laser card. By the time Rachel and I had spoken of Caram and Bola, I had already engaged Simon to take my original logo and make it look more professional. Since we served lunches to girls and boys, the most obvious colours for our double-star trademark were pink and blue.

For our characters, I felt Bola was good, but that Cara would work better than Caram. Bola is a shortened version of *boladh* which, loosely translated from Gaelic, means 'stinky'. *Cara* is the Gaelic word for 'friend'. Since we already had our double-star trademark, it seemed appropriate that the characters be shaped like stars, and that Cara should be the girl star and Bola should be the boy star. As kids said their names, they would be familiarising themselves with our brand, since 'Cara and Bola' sounds like Carambola.

Simon came up with these designs for Cara and Bola, and the kids *love* them!

What Would Michael O'Leary Do?

BC – Before Carambola – the government-sponsored lunches Irish children were fed were cheap and not so cheerful. You got ham on Monday, cheese on Tuesday, corned beef on Wednesday and, if you didn't like it, then tough. You ate it or went hungry.

Thank God we never looked at the competition when we began because, if we had, we would probably have tried to do what they were doing, only a little cheaper or faster or whatever. Instead, we asked the marketplace what it wanted and found a way to provide that.

But it wasn't initially like that. In fact, after three months, I nearly threw in the towel. Then I asked myself, 'What would Michael O'Leary do in this situation?'

We had just started and it was painful. I couldn't believe how much work was going into the preparation and delivery of twenty-seven lunches a day. We were running a café that served hundreds of meals per day, so why was this so difficult?

So I nearly stopped.

I had hoped – prayed even – that the school lunches would help pay the rent, but it was just too tough. Twenty-seven lunches were taking hours of administrative time daily. Teachers were disgruntled because they were faxing orders in each day with changes for the next day. Seven-year-old schoolchildren were ruling the roost. It was a nightmare.

So I went to see our client, Áine Cremin, the school principal in Corpus Christi NS, to see what could be done. At that meeting, I learned three things that would change the course of my life, and the way children in government-assisted food pro-grammes in Ireland would be fed forever.

The first thing I learned was that the programme under which we operated – which was called DEIS (pronounced 'desh') – funded the lunches to the tune of €1.20 per participating child per day. We were charging €1.99. The second thing was that, although the whole school qualified for funding, less than 10 percent of children were using it. The third thing was that the children who needed the programme the most came from homes where parents couldn't or wouldn't put their hands in their pockets to fund the €0.79 difference.

So I left the meeting and asked myself what Michael O'Leary would do. And the answer was simple: he would trade margin for volume.

I went back to Áine and asked whether she would allow all the children in her school to participate, if I dropped the price to €1.20 per child and took orders weekly instead of daily. She said yes. Among the advantages of this approach was that it removed any possible stigma from the programme, since all children would be able to use it – not just the 'poor' kids.

Because Áine agreed, our business grew ten-fold overnight. But more importantly, we had cracked the model. Word spread and other schools came to us looking for the service. The pilot programme was finally working for all stakeholders. Carambola Kidz looked like it might just take off.

Carambola Kidz in 2015 and Beyond

So, here we are, 16 million lunches and more than ten years later. A lot has changed.

The most obvious thing is that we are bigger than when we started: we feed more children every day; we employ more people; we service more parts of the country; our mission is clearer; we are helping more disadvantaged children; and we are helping to educate the next generation about the benefits of choosing a healthy lifestyle – and about the consequences of poor lifestyle choices.

Interestingly, with the help of competitors that have sprung up all over the country, we have made significant progress in our mission of promoting healthy-lifestyle awareness in all children. As a result of Carambola raising the bar, the standard of all school lunches in Ireland is light years ahead of where it was BC.

As the business grew, it needed strengthening at the board level. It grew well beyond a mere mom-and-pop-style business and, as such, needed to be treated differently. So in 2010, Aideen resigned as a director (though she remained a shareholder) and was replaced by Ger Dillon, our accountant, who joined the board as both shareholder and a director. This was a strategic move.

For any business to survive and thrive in post-Celtic-Tiger Ireland, it needs both a strong vision for its future and a strong foundation upon which to build. And for me, the mom-and-pop-style operation was not it. I am tremendously grateful to Aideen for her help in the early years, and for her ongoing support and confidence in me and in Carambola. But this approach separates business life and family life most of the time, and allows both to operate harmoniously.

Ger has been our accountant since 2005, and he and some of his staff – most notably Brian Meehan – have helped us steer through some very choppy waters. It was a natural choice for me to make when the time came, to invite him on board as co-director. The deal we struck regarding his shareholding was reflective of his stepping up to the plate. With Ger as a strategic partner, Carambola has recently begun to review the market in its entirety, and to see in an entirely new way the opportunities that exist. Brian Meehan joined the board as a director in 2013.

For years, Carambola Kidz has been the sponsor of the Irish Primary Principals' Network (IPPN's) Annual Conference Gala Dinner, which is held at the end of each January. IPPN boasts membership of about 3,500. When Ger came on board, he saw the opportunity to work more closely with the IPPN. Consequently, two things happened in 2012.

First, we found Pat Burke Walsh, a sociable retired DEIS principal. Pat liked us. We liked Pat. And so he joined us in September 2012, and became our principle principal liaison; he speaks their language. Second, that December, following much discussion and due diligence, Carambola Kidz was appointed as IPPN's preferred supplier of school lunches. This was a tremendous honour, a validation of what we are about as an organisation, and a recognition of all the hard work we have done over a decade in raising the standards for feeding disadvantaged children in Ireland.

I am extremely humbled by and yet proud of what Carambola has achieved. Let's see what the next decade brings.

CHAPTER 2
My Early Life

The Early Years

'It's a book, not a booook!' said Mr Kennedy, my fourth-class teacher, as he tried to correct my errant accent.

'B-b-booook,' I tried.

'Book,' he said again.

'B-b-ook,' I stuttered.

Mr Kennedy smiled and took a coin out of his pocket. I was delighted. It looked like I was getting a few bob for being good at my lessons. Instead of handing the coin to me, though, he raised it between his thumb and forefinger, lifted his hand about a foot off the desk and dropped it with a clatter onto the wooden surface – all while looking at me and smiling. I was confused. He did it again. I was doubly confused. Finally, he put me out of my misery.

'The penny has dropped young O'Brien, the penny has dropped. It's a book, not a booook,' he said.

This was Dublin in 1973. Northside Dublin, to be more exact. Coolock in Northside Dublin, if you want to be really picky. That's where I was growing up, where I was 'born, bred and butt'red' as the saying went. And all my friends ('me f-renz', in true Northside Dublinese) called this thing you're reading a 'booook', so that's what it was to me until Mr Kennedy put me right.

I was a good kid most of the time, terribly shy, with straight black hair and no frame to talk about. I was a reader too. I read booooks all the time. I was the leader of my own little gang in the estate: not the cool gang, but a gang nonetheless. We used to play kerbs at the side of our house. A fella would stand on one pavement and another would stand on the other side of the road, and they'd lob an orange plastic football across, trying to hit the opposite kerb with it so the ball would bounce back to its thrower. And the whoops of joy when it did! Periodically, we'd have to stop to let a car pass into Cameron Estate. Then our mothers would call us in for our tea, and we'd have to do our 'ecker' (our 'exercise', also known as homework) before we'd be let out again to play until it got dark or bath time arrived, whichever happened first.

And it was always sunny.

I was blessed, really. In her book *The Snowball: Warren Buffet and the Business of Life*, Alice Schroeder quotes Buffet as referring to this as 'the ovarian lottery'. In other words, my ticket allowed me to be born white, in Dublin, Ireland in 1963 to married parents who loved each other, worked hard, never went into debt, never drank or did drugs and who lived (and still do, thank God) for the pleasure of family life.

I remember sitting in the back of the car with my sisters and brothers when I was twelve, driving through Swords and listening to Mam and Dad in the front talking about selling the caravan we had and trading up to a mobile home – a mobile home, no less! I remember listening to them work through all the ifs, buts, maybes and ands associated with this major transaction. I remember being blown away by the complexity of it and saying 'Janey mac, Ma 'n Da, it's all happenin' in 1975, wha'?' Dad laughed and said, 'It's always all happening. It's just that now you are old enough to begin to understand.'

My older sister Carol, younger brother Ger and younger sister Trish were in the back with me. No such thing as a seat belt. Donal, the baby, was sitting on Ma's lap in the front. I can't even say it was special; it was just normal, our normal. It was nice.

Family Life

'What did you do today?' he asked after he came home from work, as was his custom.

She had the tea ready.

'I bought a house,' says she, nonchalantly.

He nearly choked!

She was a stunner; everybody said it. Big brown eyes, cheek-bones to die for. He couldn't believe his luck; she agreed to marry him. Doreen Stenson was so beautiful, in fact, that she had the honour of being chosen as bride of the month in June 1961. And so this stunner from Coolock married the lovable character Thomas O'Brien from Portmarnock, life stretching out before them with the promise of blissful adventure. And then us kids came along.

Carol made the two three in May 1962, with yours truly arriving less than eleven months later in March 1963, followed by Gerard in 1965, Trish in 1969 and Donal in 1971. And so two became seven. The seven have since become twenty-one through grandchildren, including a great-grandchild, Nikita, down under.

I remember being scared. I had been collected and taken to Granny Stenson's after school for the afternoon and, when it was dark, Uncle Ciaran had driven me to our new house: a semi-d on Tonlegee Road, on the corner leading to Cameron Estate. We drove for what seemed like miles. All I knew was we had driven out into the country, past trees and fields, before we finally got to the house. As we walked in, we realised that Mam and Dad were in the kitchen, which was at the end of a long corridor, or so it seemed. I don't remember anybody else being there.

The stairway leading to the darkness above was to the left of the hall. On the right were two doors almost side by side about halfway down. As I passed, I glanced in and saw nothing! Absolutely nothing! It was completely black, and so I was scared. I was only five, after all. I learned the following morning that the doors led to a sitting/dining room split by very fancy sliding doors, and the blackness was because of a midnight blue carpet with a sky-blue pattern – this *was* the late 1960s. As fate would have it, I'm writing this very chapter in that sitting room. Thankfully, the décor has moved on.

Tommy and Doreen O'Brien taught the five of us several things as children, mainly by example. In that simple semi-d, they taught us some very valuable life lessons, lessons I know have stood me well over the years:

- Work – you get nothin' for nothin'
- If you make a promise, keep it
- Your reputation is everything
- Give back
- Pray

By the way, Mam is still beautiful, Dad is still a lovable character, and they have stayed together through ups and downs, thick and thin, sickness and health, for more than fifty years now. As I write this, they are caravanning on the west coast of Australia with big sis Carol and her husband Ferg.

Primary School

Now that we had moved to 'the country' (we were two miles from our old home), we had a distance to travel to get to school. Dad was a salesman and always had a company car, but he went to work earlier than we went to school – and so we cycled.

We were like a family of ducks as we wobbled on our bikes to school. Carol, being the eldest, was always in front. Ger, being the youngest going to school, was in the middle, and I, being the other one, took up the rear. We struggled in single file down Tonlegee Road until we got to our school in Killester.

I remember Mr Kennedy, whom you met earlier, very well, and Mr Gaughran, the principal. There was a Mr Kenny and a Mrs Kelly but, after that, the memory fades. But it was a nice school.

I stayed back a year. It was sixth class. I think I was eleven and too young for secondary school. I remember crying as I cycled home on the last day of my first sixth class, realising that all my friends were gone. I was the only one going back in September. But, as it happened, that was the summer the new school was completed, so I was in the first cohort of students to attend the brand-new school on the corner of the Howth Road and Sybil Hill, opposite Killester Church. It had an upstairs! And block walls. And toilets adjacent to the classroom. Ultra modern.

So I got over myself and ended up enjoying a second run at sixth class. Actually, one of the great things about repeating was you got to do cool stuff because you had learned your lessons a year earlier. I remember being sent to the Gestetner and churning out copy after copy of some of teacher's work by turning a large handle so that a drum filled with noxious chemicals could 'print' from the original. The Gestetner was a forerunner of the photocopier.

Another cool thing as a retread was running the school shop. Cupboard, actually. We sold pencils and rubbers and sharpeners and compasses and copies and Moro bars. I remember Moro bars with their unique peanuty flavour.

Then my bike was stolen, and I was gutted. It was the one day I had forgotten to bring my lock and, when I came out of school, there it was – gone. I've no idea how I got home that day, but I know I got into big trouble.

Mam herself cycled for years. She always said, 'Never a borrower, nor a lender be.' And, 'If you make a pound, only spend nine shillings.' In other words, always live within your means. She used to cycle to Kilbarrack Shopping Centre and strap the 'messages' (groceries) to the baby seat on the back and then cycle home – hail, rain or shine.

Looking back, the loss of my bike would have been major for them. It was a cash society; there were no credit cards. So you either had it or you did without. And often, mam and dad did without to ensure us kids had enough.

Even Santa Claus was inventive back then. He made cowboy and Indian suits out of old curtains my mother had taken down, and he even fixed up and painted a trike that had been lying in the garage one year. Clever Santa.

Secondary School

After nine years in primary school, it was time to move on. So I entered St Paul's College, Raheny, and Mam and Dad were so proud. Their son in St Paul's: this was big time. Of course, I never knew that. Kids don't think about stuff, they simply get on with it. But apparently the folks were very proud.

There were two exciting things about going to St Paul's. One, it had a swimming pool – posh! Two, the 'caf' (cafeteria) at the pool sold chips! Could life get any better? We had no money for chips, so that part didn't really matter, but it was cool to think that that stuff was available in a *school*.

I do remember thinking that secondary school gave me a chance to reinvent myself. I had been a wimp in primary school, and I remember consciously deciding not to be as I started in first year. These boys didn't know me from Adam, nor I them, so I could really become whomever I wanted. So, overall, secondary school was a good time for me.

Oh, and girls were invented. Yep, sometime in the mid-1970s, girls showed up on Earth. Fascinating creatures that wrecked your head and caused you to lose concentration. The early school discos were lavish affairs. Baths had to be taken, hair blow-dried to within an inch of its life, and clothes chosen: elephant flares, platform shoes and, my favourite, a brown-and-white-check short jacket with faux-sheepskin lining and a huge collar. Bee's knees stuff!

Then my new mates and I would pile in to the rec hall, which had been cleared except for the DJ's table and some really funky flashing green, red and yellow lights. And the girls were there.

And everybody danced. Danced, that is, until the DJ said, 'OK, folks, we're goin' to slow it down.' And it was like someone let off a stink bomb – the floor cleared! I remember my first 'lurch', a dreadful term for a boy and a girl slow dancing with their heads on each others' shoulders, looking at everybody else 'lurching' looking at them. It still makes me shudder.

Then came The Grove years. The Grove was the Northside mecca for all us self-respecting pseudo-hippies. It was a rock disco, and Cecil was the DJ. He played every Saturday and Sunday for twenty-five years! Generations of us were reared on The Grove. Ah, good times.

The 'Inter' (Intermediate Certificate) exams in fourth year were a big deal, although they were really only preparation for the 'Leavin' two years later. Between those two exams was fifth year and, for me, that was the best year ever. Remember those girls I told you about? Well, our school and a local girls' school called Manor House, in Raheny, joined forces in fifth year to put on an end-of-year musical called 'Sing Out', loosely based on a global phenomenon emanating from the States called Up with People. So here we were, sixteen or seventeen years old, given the opportunity to rehearse *with real girls* for what seemed like months on end, and all we had to do was put on a show for the rest of our school mates and all the parents. I had a ball.

And to top it all off, I was fortunate enough to be one of twelve boys and twelve girls to get on the annual school trip to Europe: Norway, Sweden, Denmark, Germany, Belgium, France, England; three weeks, two mini-buses IR £155 all-in; a life-expanding experience. Thanks St Paul's. Thanks Mam and Dad.

What Do You Want to Be When You Grow Up?

All of a sudden it was September 1979, and the end was in sight. Secondary school had been great for me. I'd reinvented myself; I was cool. I had a whole bunch of new friends, some of whom I am still in contact with today.

I had long hair and wore no uniform. As a trial, St Paul's had broken with tradition the year I started and decided to allow us to go without uniforms. Apparently, it caused problems and was reversed almost immediately, but it happened that my class year was allowed go right through secondary in our civvies – and to a confirmed pseudo-hippy that was fab, man!

The Pope came to Ireland and told two hundred thousand 'yunk people of Ireland' in Ballybrit Racecourse, County Galway, that he loved them. I was among them. I was happy, very happy. But the end was nigh. All of a sudden, 'Sing Out' was over, we were back from Europe, the Pope had gone home, and people started talking about what they wanted to be when they left school.

I had never thought that far ahead. What *was* I going to be? Fellas were talking about college and points needed and honours required in the upcoming exams to become an engineer or a doctor, or to study law. I had no idea. Careers guidance lectures were organised. Bankers were wheeled in. Smart-looking dudes in suits and ties. A hundred of us sitting in the same rec hall we'd met girls in a few years earlier – only now the mood was very different.

'Can you have long hair if you work in the bank?' asked a fella with a huge grin on his cheeky face, to thunderous applause and stomping of feet. His hair was down to his ass over his faded denim jacket. The sharp-looking bankers smiled indulgently and assured him that there were people in the bank with even longer hair than his. He sat down, hero of the moment. His name was Colm. Not me, another Colm. He went on to revolutionise the world of online monetary transactions. Props to Colm Lyon who founded Realex!

None of this was helping though. I still had no clue. And then it hit me. Around St Patrick's Day 1980, I decided what I wanted to be. Colm O'Brien would become a teacher, a primary-school-teacher. Why? Did I want to help the next generation? Did I feel I had a calling? No. Short hours, long holidays. Teaching was for me!

So I began to study. I found out about St Pat's in Drumcondra and Sion Hill in Blackrock, about how to be accepted onto their teacher-training programmes. I set my Leavin' Cert eyes on the prize. It was then that I got sick. I spent Easter 1980 in hospital with a raging fever, having been diagnosed with glandular fever, aka 'the kissing disease' (no idea how that happened). For the last six weeks of my school career, I was out of school. This was when I should have been reviewing my notes and doing mock exam papers.

I sat the Leavin' anyway. I reckoned it would be good practice. I wasn't at all nervous because I was planning to repeat. But I got good results. Almost good enough to get me into St Pat's – except for the mandatory honour in Irish, which I didn't get.

UCC (under the Clerys Clock)

'You can start on Saturday.'

Those words changed my life.

I got off the lift on the third floor of Clerys and was greeted by a six-foot-tall wooden Jolly Green Giant statue. The restaurant looked nice. Fancy metal lanterns with copper shades hung over big solid wooden tables, and chunky wooden chairs with leather seats and backs stood in neat rows. The skyline of North Dublin was clearly visible through the huge windows on two sides of the room.

I went to the service area, got a cup of tea and sat shyly towards the back of the room, facing the lift, and the back of the Jolly Green Giant. There was an incredibly dapper young man in a fancy suit, black jacket, grey waistcoat, grey pinstriped trousers, silver tie and dazzling white shirt, wearing a red carnation and standing almost to attention as he greeted people who emerged from the lift.

I was waiting for my dad. He had told me to meet him in Clerys Rooftop Restaurant because he was taking me to work with him for the day. The lift opened again. Dad exited, and it was obvious that he and Dapper Man knew each other. And then, to my horror, Dad disappeared into the kitchen. He hadn't seen me.

I was on my summer holliers, the Leavin' was done and the results were in. I hadn't got the honour in Irish and I was going to have to repeat, so a plan was hatched at home: I'd get a job for a year, repeat Irish by studying at night and become a teacher – short hours, long holidays, happy days. Simples.

I had just come from a formal interview in BHS on O'Connell Street for the illustrious position of kitchen porter. They were offering me £60 per week. So it looked like part one of the get-Colm-a-teaching-job plan was in place, and I was in Clerys to meet Dad, tell him the good news and spend the day with him.

I mentioned that Dad was the best salesman in Ireland, and he was selling for Green Isle Frozen Foods. It turns out they were doing a promotion on Jolly Green Giant corn on the cob, thus the mad-looking green fella as people got off the lift. I finished my tea and walked up to Dapper Man and shyly said, 'My dad is Tommy O'Brien and he went in there.' I pointed to the swinging door with the glass panel.

In a flash, Dapper Man whisked me through the door and into a tiny office, where Dad was talking to another giant: a large man with large eyes, wearing a blazer with a colourful tie and a mismatched breast-pocket hanky. An older man in an impeccable chef's uniform was standing there with customary cloth in hand, his hair Brylcreemed perfectly.

'This is my son, Colm. This is Mr Halpin and his partner Barney Neilan,' Dad said, as we shook hands.

'What are you doing with yourself young man?' boomed Mr Halpin.

So I told him the story: no honour in Irish, get a job, repeat the Leavin', become a teacher – happy days. And I added, 'I've just come from BHS and I got a job, £60 a week, kitchen porter.'

Dad looked suitably impressed until Mr Halpin said, 'My cashier is leaving this week; you can start on Saturday and work part-time when you go to college next year. It's £40 a week, but I'll train you. It'll be better for you than becoming a kitchen porter.'

I had a dilemma.

Anything Worth Doing
Is Worth Doing Badly

Badly, that is, until you learn to do it well. I was scared stiff. I had decided that the cashier job had more potential than kitchen portering. So I donned a jacket and tie – no suit, I had a fading hippy rep to protect – and I went to work. Dad had warned me that the guys, Mr Halpin, Barney Neilan and Declan O'Connor (aka Dapper Man), were some of the most professional in the industry. And I was about to join them. The pressure was immense.

On that first Saturday, when I got off the lift, the restaurant was empty. I was immediately greeted by a tall, very thin young man with lank hair perfectly split down the middle. He was very polite as he informed me the restaurant wasn't open yet.

'I'm starting work here today,' I blurted, much to his surprise.

'OK,' he said. 'Sort the cutlery while I make a phone call.'

Sort the cutlery? He may as well have asked me to replace the carburettor in a Volkswagen. I had a vague idea what it meant, but no clue how to do it. Sort the cutlery I did, though. Knives, forks, large spoons and teaspoons were lined up in a grey container with four purpose-built wells for the job. I sifted through the knives; they looked sorted to me. I moved then to the forks; a bit tangley, but then that's their nature. Next, it was the large spoons; some had round heads, and some were more spear-shaped but, again, they looked OK. The teaspoons were a doddle. All sorted.

I was happy as I waited for my next job. Thin Guy came back.

'I phoned Mr Halpin so now I know what's going on,' he said.

'I'm Ciaran O'Briain, the restaurant manager. Welcome aboard. I see you had no luck sorting the cutlery.'

I was gobsmacked. I must have spent ten minutes sorting it. I wanted to ask him what he meant, but I remembered my dad's warning, so I just apologised.

Ciaran then took the time to explain to me how I should have sorted the cutlery. He showed me how to remove all the knives, clean out the well and polish each knife with a soft cloth, before placing it with its handle facing the customer. The forks were next, and placing them all cupped into each other, as he instructed, made for a much neater presentation. It turned out the round spoons were soup spoons and the spear-shaped ones were dessert spoons, and they shared a well but were cupped separately. Even the teaspoons were immeasurably neater when Ciaran had finished. The pièce de résistance was when we filled the napkin dispensers that stood at either end of the grey tray with four wells housing cutlery and polished their chrome faces.

When we stood back and looked at the cutlery table, I knew we'd done a good job. My dad was right: I was in professional company.

That lesson was the first of many, many lessons in doing the job right that I was fortunate to learn while working with those four men from the age of seventeen. Looking back, I was blessed to find myself in their company. Each of them had a profound impact on who I became over the years.

So, there I was, enjoying working in Clerys Rooftop Restaurant six days a week, and studying Irish at night. I had money in my pocket: £40 a week was a lot for someone who regularly had cut an entire lawn for 50p! The plan was working. Roll on next summer, repeat the Leavin', go to college, become a teacher – short hours, long holidays. Happy days.

Carry the Customer's Tray

But the Man Upstairs had a different plan.

I started working in the food industry by accident. I learned quickly. I enjoyed it. And when you enjoy something and are willing to work hard and learn, you get good at it. And when you get good at something, you get ahead. And so it went for me.

'You could make a career out of this,' Mr Halpin said, landing in a seat next to me at my first Christmas party with his company.

I didn't quite know what to say. I certainly was enjoying myself. I hate to admit it, but I smoked at the time, and my wages allowed for ten cigs a day (twenty on a Saturday), a few drinks, zero responsibility and good fun. I found it hard to imagine giving up my new income to go to college. The Irish grinds in Mr Craven's house had become just that – a grind. My teaching plan was losing its lustre.

'I'm opening a new restaurant in the ILAC Centre next year, and a guy like you could go far,' Mr Halpin said.

So the die was cast. By Christmas 1980, I had binned the idea of teacher-training college. I retired from the Irish grinds and I got stuck in to an industry that offered the complete opposite to primary teaching. I had lined myself up for a career of long hours and short holidays. Funny old rock 'n' roll world. But I believe it was meant to be.

I loved it. I became great at my job. We were flying as a company. The ILAC Centre opened as the most modern shopping centre in Ireland in 1981, and Hallins Restaurant opened with me as a trainee manager. I had graduated to wearing the morning suit, complete with silver tie and fresh red carnation. I looked the part.

Mr Halpin was ahead of his time. He and Barney Neilan had worked at Dublin's Gresham Hotel, back when the Gresham was the Gresham, if you know what I mean, and exceptional service was where it was at. They created an entirely unique restaurant experience in both Clerys and the ILAC. Both were traditional (at the time) self-service restaurants, where you picked up a tray, slid it along a rail past the desserts, salads, confectionery, hot counter, beverage counter and cash register, and then took it to find a seat. In the early 1980s, the typical self-service experience was all too often second-rate. Halpin and Neilan raised the bar significantly; they carried the customer's tray to the table.

As a service, it set us apart from the competition; as a tool in our trade, it allowed us to manage and optimise our seating lay-out, guaranteeing faster throughput and more-satisfied clients.

I became great at carrying the customer's tray. In fact, I was superb at it. Carrying the customer's tray exceeded the customer's expectation by a mile. It guaranteed satisfaction and, most importantly, return custom. It was a winning formula.

Carrying the customer's tray taught me that, when it's all boiled down, exceptional service will win the day. So I made a decision circa 1985 that, even though Mr Halpin paid my wages, I would consider myself self-employed. I decided that, from that moment on, I was effectively working for me – I would become the best in my field.

Something Had to Change

'Is that your own milk madam?' I asked the horrified young mother.

She was pushing a buggy with a newborn whilst attempting to balance her self-service tray, on which stood a baby's bottle three-quarters full of white liquid. From her disgusted look, I instantly realised I had made a mistake. We often sold parents glasses of milk they could pour into their babies' bottles. I had simply intended to clarify whether the cashier should charge for the milk, or whether the woman had brought it from home.

I was mortified! But that's what happens when you're learning your trade.

The service was so good in our restaurants in the mid-1980s that we were awarded several national Bord Fáilte Awards for it. It was a heady time. But then things began to change for me. One of the problems with the Clerys/Hallins formula was that it required huge personal, physical efforts by a few key people – myself included. And by 1987, I was tired.

I met Aideen in 1984, and we fell in love. A beauty from Mullingar, Aido had moved to Dublin several years earlier to be a civil servant. She worked Monday to Friday; I worked six days a week, with Saturday being by far the busiest. When I'd get home late Saturday evening, I'd just fall asleep, which was not very romantic. I began to resent not having enough time to spend with her. Despite all that, we married in January 1986 and were blessed with the birth of Shóna later that same year. After that, the pressure was really on. My earning potential was limited in Mr Halpin's company. Something had to change.

All this time, I was convinced that I was an interloper, that I really had no right to be a caterer, because *real* caterers had college backgrounds. So I decided to enrol in an evening diploma course in supervisory management at DIT, Cathal Brugha Street. That is when I learned the big secret! Want to know it? The big secret is . . . there is no big secret. *Nobody* has all the answers. I was learning in college the theory of what I was practicing every day; college simply validated my field knowledge. Realising that I had as much right as anyone else in the food industry gave me the courage to look for another job. And, as luck would have it, I was offered two.

Having taken the bold step of sending out a CV, I was offered two jobs. One was as the deputy manager of Bewley's on Grafton Street, for £12,000 a year. The other was as the manager of a small café in Blackrock Shopping Centre for £14,000 a year, plus a small percentage of turnover. At the time, I was earning £12,000 a year plus a bonus, so the Blackrock job was the most logical opportunity for a newly married man with a mortgage to pay, nappies to buy and car payments to make. But I chose Bewley's. It was a backward step, financially, but I have never done anything for money – I'm more interested in what I can learn. And I felt that I could learn more and grow more in the ever-expanding Campbell Bewley Group.

Once again, I was scared stiff. My mouth was dry for the first week in my new job, but soon I began to feel at home. Mary Devlin was my manager, a dynamo from Northern Ireland who made me feel welcome. Very quickly, she and I became a terrific team, working together in that 'legendary, lofty, clattery café'.[1]

---

1. Brendan Kennelly, quoted in Tony Farmar's 1988 book *The Legendary Lofty Clattery Café: Bewley's of Ireland.*

The Legendary, Lofty, Clattery Café

'Dublin's legendary, lofty, clattery café has been one of Ireland's best-loved meeting places for over a century. Actors, lovers, poets and politicians from near and far come to Bewley's, to meet and mingle in one of Ireland's favourite cafés.'

—Brendan Kennelly

My years at Bewley's on Grafton Street were, in the main, fantastic. All of life was found within its walls. It was the de facto centre of life in Dublin, and I was privileged to carry the baton for a short few years in its long, illustrious history. I became general manager in 1991, when I was twenty-eight, and remained so until 1995.

With the help of some really great staff, many of whom were lifers, some of whom were second- and even third-generation Bewley's staff, we managed to transform the way the café operated, making it easier for people to come in, be helped to their seats and get served quickly – all the stuff I had learned with Mr Halpin. The champagne came out when the café hit £100,000 in a week for the first time. I was home!

Two changes were implemented in my time at Bewley's on Grafton Street that have survived the test of time. One was that we began staying open later. It sounds obvious now but, back in the early 1990s, it wasn't. At that time, Bewley's closed at 6 PM because, well, that's the way it had always been. I remember leaving the building at 6 PM one summer evening and realising that Grafton Street was thronged. I rang Paddy Campbell, chairman of the group, and suggested we stay open until 10 PM the following summer. A few days later, he rang back and said, 'Let's go to 1 AM!' So we did.

I have vivid memories of standing at the front door at midnight, cajoling pub- and club-goers to come in, convincing them that we were, in fact, open for business. They didn't believe it for a while, but once word got out, man, what an explosion of new business! We kept extending the hours until we were completely full between 3 AM and 4 AM! Crazy stuff, but all good. One of the most fascinating elements of this was that there such respect for the institution by the people who came in; there was never any damage done to it intentionally.

Bewley's on Grafton Street became a place to go for breakfast (before bed), a place to while away the night-time hours with friends, to engage in convivial conversations over bacon, eggs, sausages, Bewley's brown bread and mugs of white Bewley's coffee. It was magical. These days, it remains open until 10 PM Sunday to Wednesday, and until 11 PM Thursday to Saturday.

The second change came about when two women walked in, introduced themselves as actresses, and said they had a play set in a coffee shop. They asked whether they could show it at Bewley's. I recognised one of them, Bairbre Ní Chaoimh, from the telly. A good idea, I thought, so I led them to the Oriental Room on the second floor, a small function room with its own kitchen. They thought it was perfect. And so Bewley's Café Theatre began. Soup, sandwich and a show for a set price. In and out between 1 PM and 2 PM. Legends such as Maeve Binchy and Christy Moore showcased works there. When I brought my youngest daughter there at Christmas in 2012, I was particularly pleased to see that the initiative had led to the venue remaining an important part of the Dublin theatre scene, even twenty years later. And it looks like it will continue to go from strength to strength under the auspices of a board tasked with its development.

CHAPTER 3

A Man on a Ladder, an Ice-Hockey Player, a Hedgehog and a Vietnam Vet

Lookin' Good

By the early 1990s things were looking up for me and Aido. I was the general manager of Bewley's on Grafton Street, the busiest, most famous, café in Ireland, with a staff approaching two hundred, supported by a management team of twenty. I was supporting the lot, and I was only twenty-eight.

This time I wasn't nervous. I knew what I was doing by then and was comfortable with my own ability to lead the team. Since joining Bewley's in 1988, I had held several roles. Initially, I was deputy manager of Bewley's on Grafton Street. Stupidly, I left after six months to go work for a start-up – better described as an 'upstart' – café company. This was a bad move, and I crawled back to Bewley's within six months, suitably embarrassed. Paddy Campbell forgave my naivety, but I was back as a line manager, not the deputy manager as before.

Bewley's opened its first ever Northside café, on Mary Street, and I was put in charge of the catering side. I did that, enjoyed it and learned from it. Then, as happens in all large and growing organisations, there was movement at the top and opportunity arose. I was handed the reins at the flagship café. At the ceremony in 1991 to announce the changes, I was thrilled to get a cheer from some of the staff, including the union's local shop steward. *This was going to be great*, I thought. And it was – for a while.

If it looks good, smells good and sounds good . . . it might not be. To the outsider, life looked good for Aido and me: new home in Celbridge, two cars, two kids (Steven joined us in 1992), good jobs (Aido worked in a bank). But the reality was a mortgage, car payments and nappies, and I was still working incredibly long hours.

Once again, I was tired of it all.

I'm not proud of it but, in my thirtieth year, I began to resent my life. I realised that I had never really planned ahead, I had always gone with the flow and I woke up one day realising that if I didn't take control of it, life would pass me by. I was blessed, really. I had two kids, two cars, a mortgage and a very good job. Many would think I had it all. But I felt that I did not have the life I wanted, so something had to change.

I mentioned earlier in this book that I love Christmas, but that wasn't always the case. Well, perhaps that's not true. I probably always did, but in the early 1990s, I had begun to *hate* what Christmas meant in the catering industry. Christmas Eve was always the busiest day of the year. My day would begin at about 6 AM and, after holding the place together for twelve or thirteen hours, I would limp home to Aido and the kids: Mass, bath time, jammies, bed, kids who couldn't sleep – all excited about Santa. When they were finally asleep, Aido and I would sip a glass of wine and crawl off after them.

'He *came!*' was the cry as two wide-eyed kids found their Christmas presents. 'Oh, no!' I used think, as I crawled out of bed way too early to celebrate my one and only day off for Christmas. Then it was presents, breakfast, play with the kids, dinner, another glass of wine, kids off to bed, sleep on the couch, to bed early and back to work again on St Stephen's Day. Another year in the trenches.

I began to realise that all I was really qualified to do was work hard in a relentless, unforgiving industry. I really had to get a grip on my life. But how?

The Power of the Network

I never knew I was an orphan until he called.

Not a real orphan, obviously, but an insurance orphan. Apparently, I had a policy with Canada Life, and the agent that 'owned' me had left the company, so I was passed to a new local man in my new area of Celbridge, County Kildare. I was in the kitchen in Celbridge when he arrived to explain that he was now my new support agent. Grand. No problem. But then, over a cup of tea, he asked if I was open to looking at new ways of making money.

'Of course,' I replied. 'Isn't everybody?'

So he began to explain the power of a thing called 'network marketing'. I was impressed with how a network could expand exponentially, the basic premise being that I would recruit five people into my network and help them recruit five each (twenty-five) and help them recruit five each (one hundred twenty-five) and so on. Seemed logical to me, and so I went to a meeting.

There must have been fifty people at the Lucan Spa Hotel that night, a week later, when I arrived to hear about the 'opportunity'. Drinking water from the tap was losing its appeal as the bottled-water industry grew, and the National Safety Associates (NSA) product range proposed to allow people the benefits of bottled water directly from special drinking taps fitted to their kitchen sinks, attached to filter units neatly hidden where the cleaning agents are normally kept. And each person in my network would sell water filters, and we'd all make money.

The plan seemed sound, and the product seemed like a good one, so I got involved and, for the first time in my life, I was in business for myself. Part-time, at least. I still had a day job. I was excited. But it didn't work for me. I understand it has worked for others, but I wasn't to be one of them. I learned a lot, however. I learned about water and filters and plumbing and how to make sales calls and how not to make sales calls. Mostly, I learned a lot about me. I learned that I can be tenacious when I want to be. I learned that nothing is easy, but that that is OK. I learned a lot about rejection.

I was utterly convinced about the potential of building that elusive network, but I realised that, for me, it wouldn't be with NSA. So I left NSA and joined Amway. That was far more interesting. Two of the elements that were significantly better in Amway were: 1) the support network, i.e. the people 'above me', and the training they offered; and 2) the product range, which consisted of, ironically, those same cleaning materials that were under the sinks where I had been trying to install water filters. Amway didn't work for me either, though.

Now, the sharper reader might see a pattern here. Perhaps the problem was, er, me? And maybe it was but, if so, *c'est la vie*, I have no regrets. I gave my foray into network marketing a full decade, but couldn't get it to work for me. I think perhaps it wasn't *meant* to be for me.

In fact, I will be eternally grateful that my personal journey led me to network marketing, in general, and to the training system offered by my 'upline' in Amway, in particular. It was second to none and utterly life changing. It was built on three elements that can be pivotal to success in any field: books, tapes and meetings. Through the power of the network, I saw the potential of leveraging my own efforts by learning to work with and through others.

Education Is the Key

Who remembers the Walkman?

Of course, you are showing your age here. If you don't know what a Walkman is and you have to Google it, then you are young enough to be my child or grandchild. The Sony Walkman was the iPod or smartphone of its day, a revolution in mobile listening technology. It played cassettes, or 'tapes', on which recordings had been made. Most were professional recordings but a lot were pirate copies. Back in the day, though, pirate copies were copies one made for one's mates, not dodgy versions sold from the backs of vans. The pirates involved more closely resembled kids in Halloween costumes than the villains and charlatans that abound today.

In the 1980s and 1990s, the Walkman – like the iPod or smartphone today – was used by all sorts of people to listen to all sorts of stuff. Then, as now, however, most people wearing headphones and walking down the street or travelling on trains or buses were listening to music: either their own selections or perhaps via their favourite radio stations. Of course, back in the Walkman era, listening to your own selection meant listening to an entire album from an individual artist or band.

You could fast-forward on all versions of the Walkman and rewind on some, so if you wanted to change tracks, you would hit 'FF', wait and *guess* when to stop! To listen to another artist meant changing tapes. But, do you know what? It was great. It wasn't glamorous, but it worked. It was mobile and it was cutting-edge at the time. In fact, I saw a great photo on the Internet showing a Walkman and an iPod decked out in Star Wars costumes. The Walkman had a speech bubble: 'I am your father!'

In the mid-1970s, my dad, whom you met earlier, did his Leaving Cert as a proud thirty-seven-year-old. By his own admission, he had run out of school as soon as he'd been old enough. But he was big enough to admit, years later, that he'd made a mistake, so he enrolled in adult education. I was twelve or thirteen at the time, and was aware that he was studying at the kitchen table late at night.

Dad also conceived a genius plan to revise as he travelled the highways and byways of Ireland, selling his wares. The Walkman had not been invented yet, but he recorded his notes and played them from a portable cassette player about the size of a Wii console, which he stowed under the seat in his car. He said that, when he sat in the exam hall and read a question, he could 'hear' the click of the recorder and the hiss of the tape and the sound of his own voice, recounting what he had learned. He passed the Leavin'. So here I was, in my thirties, utilising a technique I had seen my dad use almost a quarter of a century earlier: listening to tapes on the go.

You see, the Amway training philosophy was based on the simple, but not widely known, philosophy that 'your business can never outgrow you'. Think about it. It's not possible for it to be any other way. For my business to grow, *I* had to grow. So I enrolled in the Book of the Month Club and the Tape of the Week Club. But *much* more important than enrolling, I participated. I listened to a personal-development tape every week and read a book every month. Listening to motivational tapes and reading a personal-development book every month has provided me with more long-term benefits than anything else I have done in my life.

A Man on a Ladder

It was one of those beautiful mornings in Dublin. You know the type. The sun was shining, the sky was blue, seagulls were circling above the Liffey and the smell of the Guinness hops roasting in St James's Gate Brewery hung heavy in the air as the double-decker bus I was on shunted down the quays from Heuston Station in rush-hour traffic. The year was 1991, and bus lanes hadn't arrived in Ireland yet.

I was listening to the Walkman I introduced you to earlier. Like a lot of people back then, I had my headphones on to block out the outside world. Then, as now, headphones were worn by many different types of people: students, joggers, walkers, business people and mothers with buggies. Then, as now, most people were listening to their favourite music. Then, as now, only a few people were using this amazing mobile technology to study. I was one of those few.

So there I was, minding my own business, using the necessary evil of rush-hour traffic to my advantage by turning otherwise-wasted time into a tremendous opportunity to expand my thinking. I can't remember specifically what I was listening to that morning, but I know it was to do with business: the dos and don'ts, the whys and why nots, the thinking that takes you forward vs. the thinking that keeps you stuck in a rut. I was enjoying the morning en route to my stop at O'Connell Bridge, from which I would make my way across the river, up Westmoreland Street and around College Green to Bewley's on Grafton Street to start work.

The bus shuddered to a stop at some traffic lights and, outside the window, I saw him: the man on the ladder.

He was an older man, and he moved with the ease of someone who had known his trade for many years. He was washing a first-floor window by leaning from a rung high up on the ladder, trusting his safety to a teenage-looking boy holding the ladder securely at ground level. But when I looked more closely, I realised that the young fella was, in fact, leaning back onto the ladder, one leg on the ground, the other leg crooked over the first rung, arms crossed like he hadn't a worry in the world as he looked across the Liffey.

And I made a judgement. Based on what I was learning about business, I judged that the man was self-employed and the young fella was his son. I assumed he was the best window cleaner in the world and that his clients, of whom there were many, were very happy with him. So, what was the problem? Well, none really. Except for the fact that, regardless of how good he was at washing windows, there were only so many windows he could wash in a day. His earning capacity was limited to his personal physical effort and was only sustainable should he remain fit for window washing. If it rained, he couldn't wash windows. When it got dark, his earning for the day finished. If he got sick or took a holiday, no windows would be washed and no income would be earned.

Millions of people are self-employed, and most of them are very happy and grateful to be, but it really wasn't where I wanted to go. I knew this, but I didn't know why until a Vietnam vet explained it to me years later.

Dancing on Ice

Back in the day, as a senior manager with the Campbell Bewley Group, I was privileged to attend some group training-and-development sessions, all of which I thoroughly enjoyed, and some of which held life-long lessons for me.

Paddy Campbell, the hands-on chairman of the group, often led such sessions and, at one point, he introduced us to a Canadian ice-hockey player. And this wasn't just any Canadian ice-hockey player. It was a hall-of-famer by the name of Wayne Gretzky.

Nicknamed the Great One, Wayne Douglas Gretzky has been called 'the greatest hockey player ever' by sportswriters, players and even the NHL. He is the leading point-scorer in NHL history and is the only NHL player to total over two hundred points in one season – a feat he accomplished four times. In addition, he tallied over one hundred points in sixteen professional seasons, fourteen of them consecutive. At the time of his retirement in 1999, aged thirty-eight, he held forty regular-season records, fifteen playoff records, and six all-star records. In addition to being its greatest scorer, Gretzky was the most gentlemanly superstar in the modern history of the NHL. He won the Lady Byng Trophy for sportsmanship and performance five times, and he often spoke out against fighting in hockey.

But, what has this got to do with business? Lots really.

You see, you don't get great by accident. It takes work – hard work – and lots of it, over a sustained period of time. Wayne Gretzky honed his skills over many years. He donned his first pair of skates at three and played on his first team when he was six. Gretzky was a hard worker and a quick learner.

One of the quotes he is famous for was actually first uttered by his father Walter: 'Skate to where the puck is going, not to where it has been.'

This is sage advice for all of us in business. Skating to where the puck is going to be is analogous for positioning our business-es to take advantage of where the market will be in two, three or five years, so that we are 'in place' when it arrives. This is far more efficient than chasing it all over the place as it meanders.

'You miss 100 percent of the shots you don't take' is another Gretzky nugget. It has a ring of stating-the-obvious about it, but the obvious is usually only obvious after you hear someone else say it. Anyway, think about that Gretzky-ism for a moment. What will happen if, after reading this book and/or doing a Start Your Own Business (SYOB) course, you decide to put the books away and not take a shot at your own thing? The answer is obvi-ous. Nothing. *Nothing* changes. You chose not to take a shot, and we now know, thanks to a Canadian ice-hockey player, what hap-pens if you don't take a shot. No shot, no goal.

What will happen if you *do* take a shot and start your busi-ness? Who knows? It might work (you might score) and it might not (you might miss), but if you don't take a shot, the result is 100 percent predictable. You miss 100 percent of the time.

Hedgehog for Breakfast

It's early morning and Little Hedgehog is out and about doing what hedgehogs do best, which is mooching for food. They mooch through hedges and other undergrowth in search of the small creatures that compose the bulk of their diet: insects, worms, centipedes, snails, mice, frogs and snakes. As a hedgehog picks its way through the hedges it emits pig-like grunts – thus the name.

Hedgehogs have a unique feature. They have coats of stiff, sharp spines. If attacked, they will curl into prickly, unappetising balls that deter most predators. They usually sleep in this position during the day and awaken to search for food at night.

The fox wants hedgehog for breakfast so he gets up early, before it gets light, stands to the right of a hole in the hedge, and waits. Little Hedgehog is oblivious and continues mooching. The gap between the two shrinks by the minute.

All of a sudden, Little Hedgehog's hog-sense begins tingling. Something is not right, so he does what has been programmed into his DNA: he curls up just in time to evade the jaws of the lunging fox. Foxy gets pricked, lets out a yelp and shoots off to rethink his strategy for having a hedgehog breakfast the next day. Little Hedgehog waits patiently until his hog-sense says the coast is clear and continues mooching towards the dawn and bed for the day. Happy life.

You see, the hedgehog is the best in the world at . . . being a hedgehog. He knows what he's about. He knows what he's not about. He doesn't try to be something he can never be. He'll never be a fox, and no amount of personal development books, tapes and seminars will change that. He's content with his lot.

What's this about? I hear you cry. Has O'Brien lost the run of himself? This is about two things. Knowing what you are about and being the best in the world at it. And the corollary is equally important: knowing what you are not about.

The story of the hedgehog and the fox provides a very important lesson, in terms of us in our businesses. The 'hedgehog' concept of business, from *Good to Great* by Jim Collins, asks us to ask ourselves three important questions about what we are doing.

1. Can you be the best in the world at it?

Now, the world, when you begin a business, may simply be the area you live in – your town or county or your region of the country – but, of course, some businesses today are 'born global' online, with immediate worldwide reach. Regardless, you are being asked whether you can be the best in the world, not whether you can be as good as yer man down the road, who you're planning to copy. Little Hedgehog has high standards.

2. Are you passionate about it?

If you're not, don't start. It really will be too much work. Remain an employee. Regardless of how hard you think you are working for your boss, you will work markedly harder when you have your own business.

3. What drives your economic engine?

This subject is for another day but, at some point, you will have to identify one piece of information, the measurement of which will satisfy you that your business is in good health.

Helicopters Don't Glide

The engine died. Not in a van in the wilds of Mayo this time, but at height above the South China Sea, in a helicopter belonging to the US Marine Corps. This was bad. The pilot and his co-pilot looked at each other for a second and realised that it was not a training exercise, it was real. They were part of the air-support detail for an American mission into Vietnam, and their job was to help provide a safe perimeter around an aircraft carrier. Robert Kiyosaki, a Japanese-American from Hawaii and his co-pilot were going down. Can you imagine it?

A helicopter is controlled by a stick. Pull back and it goes up, push forward and it goes down; left is left and right is right. But the training they had received for such an emergency was 100 percent counter-intuitive. I believe you will agree with me that the most natural thing to do in Kiyosaki's situation would be to pull the stick back with all your might. I can even imagine myself putting my feet on the windshield to get extra leverage! But no, Kiyosaki, as the man in charge, pushed forward, as he had been trained to. He didn't want to, but he did.

You see, helicopters don't glide. They, well, fall. Pushing for-ward on the stick means the front of your helicopter will fall first, allowing you gather air speed as you plummet to earth or, in this case, ocean. (Told you it was counter-intuitive!) Why, in God's name, would you want to gather speed? To survive, believe it or not. You see, as you gather speed in a helicopter, it affords you some control so that, just before you are about to hit, you can pull back on the stick and, miracle of miracles, the chopper will level out, giving you a greater chance of survival. The boys lived.

It is this same Robert Kiyosaki who I was introduced to as part of an Amway book-of-the-month club, and his teachings have radically informed who I have become and the journey I find myself on today. I am very happy to recommend his Rich Dad Series and, in particular, Rich Dad's Cashflow Quadrant: Guide to Financial Freedom. But, if you are planning to read it, for context, you should start with the first book in the series: Rich Dad, Poor Dad: What the Rich Teach Their Kids About Money – That the Poor and Middle Class Do Not.

In Cashflow Quadrant, Kiyosaki presents the four types of players in the business world like this:

1. Employees	3. Business Owners
2. The Self-employed	4. Investors

Everybody in the business world falls into one or more of these categories, which are not mutually exclusive. For example, I might work for McDonald's (employee) and dabble in shares or property (investor) and perhaps DJ at weekends (self-employed).

For me, the most significant lesson in the *Cashflow Quadrant* was not what each player does, but rather the difference between those categories on the left side and those on the right side. Kiyosaki explains that employees and the self-employed *trade* their time for money, whereas business owners and investors *leverage* time and/or money.

Finally, I knew why I didn't want to be self-employed. I didn't want to *trade* time. I wanted to live on the right side of the quadrant. Where are you today? Where do you want to be in five years?

The Leverage Factor

'You'd make a fortune in your own little coffee shop.'

Friends and family regularly told me this for years, based on my obvious talent in the front-of-house side of the coffee-shop industry. Let's face it, I was good – possibly great. That's not ego speaking; I had a knack and it showed. So the most obvious thing for people to advise was that I open my own 'little' coffee shop. But I was never tempted, and I couldn't figure out why until I read Robert Kiyosaki's books.

When he explained the difference between the left-hand and right-hand sides of the Cashflow Quadrant, it was as if a light went on or, as my old schoolteacher Mr Kennedy put it, the penny dropped! Finally I realised there *was* a difference between being self-employed and being a business owner, that the two are worlds apart. I realised I wanted to live on the right-hand side of the quadrant.

The only place to start was from where I was, and the first step was to get a clear picture in my mind of the four types of players in the world of business, so here is what I came up with:

1. Employees

This is an easy one for most people to understand. As an employee, you work a defined role and get paid by the hour, week or month, PAYE and/or commission, bonus or no bonus. You get paid by someone who hired you to help them do their work. When you work, you get paid; when you don't work, you don't. If you leave your job, your pay ceases. The leverage factor is one.

2. The Self-employed

A man with a ladder and a bucket who is willing to knock on doors can make a living as a self-employed window cleaner. He will trade his time for money. If he is not washing windows, he can't earn. Everything from bad weather to vacation time can impact his earning capacity. The leverage factor is one.

3. Business Owners

A business owner is someone who owns or controls a business system that operates at least in part without the owner. Take, for example, Michael O'Leary (Ryanair, about 9,000 employees in 2013) and Richard Branson (Virgin Group, about 50,000 employees in 2014). Their leverage factors are at least in line with the number of employees who work for their companies – 9,000 to 50,000 – not to mention potential financial leverage.

4. Investors

Warren Buffet is arguably the Western world's most famous investor. As of November 2014, he is the world's third-richest man, with an estimated fortune of $50 billion. How did he do it? Well, he bought a company and leveraged it by taking the profits and buying another company and leveraged that other company by taking the profits and buying another company, and kept on like that. Can you see where this is going? He owns hundreds of companies. In March 2014, Buffet's wealth increased by more than $1 billion (yes, billion) in just twenty-two hours, according to *Forbes*. His leverage factor is, well, enormous!

Obviously, I've simplified the transactions/concepts above, but I hope you get the idea. The same leverage opportunity I saw in network marketing exists through building traditional business-es. I know now that this is my personal route.

The Man with the Big Kidneys

'Here he comes: the man with the big kidneys,' said my mother.

At first, I thought she was talking about someone else, and I was tempted to look behind myself to see who was following me, and what sort of disfigurement the poor soul was suffering from. But she was talking to me about me.

Confused, I asked her what she meant, and she explained that, when she was growing up in Rialto and then Coolock, the term 'big kidneys' was used to describe someone who thought above his station – someone with big dreams. Instead of being offended, I chose to accept that as a compliment. I am the man with the big kidneys. I always ask why life can't be bigger, better, brighter today than it was yesterday. And bigger, better, brighter again tomorrow.

There is, perhaps, a more sinister side to the phrase 'the man with the big kidneys'. We Irish are great *craic* (fun) in the main. We are known the world over for many things, including our laissez-faire attitude to life: the 'sure, it'll be grand' philosophy. But when it comes to the man or woman with the big kidneys, with dreams, who believes he or she can get ahead, that same 'sure, it'll be grand' way of thinking can all too often be replaced by, 'Who does he think he is?'

'Sure it'll be grand' only works when we all subscribe to it, when we all stay in the same pool and respect the same pecking order. So, if you get above your station, all of a sudden, people start saying, 'Sure, he's not the same as he used to be. He's changed.' And they often say it like it's a bad thing! There is a saying that, when our American cousins see the man or woman getting ahead, living in the big house on the hill, they say, 'Someday, I'm going to live like that.' In Ireland, we can be known to say, 'Someday, I'm going to get that fecker.'

My dad, the best salesman in Ireland, worked hard all his life to put bread on the table. He felt privileged to have a job and a company car – he always had a company car – and he had reason to. When he grew up in Portmarnock, he never knew wealth of any kind. His own dad, my grandfather, was a 'traveller', not in the sense of being a part of the Travelling community, but in the sense of being a 'traveller' for a company, hawking wares the length and breadth of the country, gone Monday to Friday. In relative terms, Dad had 'made it'. We had a nice roof over our heads, food on the table, love in the cupboards – all the important stuff.

So, here I am, by my own mother's admission, the man with the big kidneys. I am not happy to settle for 'my station' in life. But, because getting a job and being grateful for it was all I knew from my genealogy, I had to learn anything beyond that from somewhere else. And that's what I began to do. I realised at age thirty that I wasn't getting ahead, I was still working for somebody else. Yes, I was grateful, but I felt there had to be more. There had to be a way to look at life differently.

I began to ask questions.

Why did some people get ahead?

Why did some of those get further ahead than others?

What made a Richard Branson a Richard Branson?

What was a business owner, anyway?

Could I be one?

I eventually realised that I did not want to be self-employed, but I would love to own a business.

'Choose Wisely, Grasshopper'

Kung Fu was a TV series in the 1970s. As a pupil learning the art of kung fu at a monastery, a very young David Carradine played the lead character. Calling him by a pet name, his 'master' told him, 'Choose wisely, Grasshopper.' Sage advice indeed.

We are asked to decide in school what we want to be when we grow up, and then remain locked into the path we choose. I feel this is a flawed system. It's flawed because we don't have the information we need to make such important choices at such a young age.

Let's take the 'A' student who chooses medicine – a very worthy, noble calling. She studies hard for the Leavin' to get enough points; seven 'A's will probably do it. Then she gets to go to college for up to six years before she starts to earn a living in her chosen career. And, as an intern, she may work up to a hundred hours a week to learn on the job. If she survives that, yes, she can earn six figures, but it will be in a high-stress environment, and she must turn up every day for the next forty years to generate said six-figure income.

Now, please don't take this out of context. I am not knocking any particular career path or calling. I am just highlighting a fact I believe to be true: people, particularly school-leavers, choose careers without having enough information about all the different ways there are to earn a living – as an employee, a self-employed person, a business owner, or an investor. Why is this? Because, by their very nature, schoolteachers have jobs, are employees and logically can only advise on that line.

I fell into this same trap. I had well-meaning people, most of whom loved me (i.e. family and friends), offering me the best advice they could based on their own paradigms – how they saw the world. The best I could hope for was to get a good job, work hard and, hopefully, retire within forty-five or fifty years. So that's what I set out to do. But then, at thirty, I realised that, for me, that was a mug's game and, unless I took control, life would control me forever.

My dilemma was that I didn't want to be an employee and I didn't want to be self-employed, either. So what was left? I could be a business owner or an investor. So I chose to become a business owner. I had to start somewhere. But where?

And then a series of events showed me my path. A good friend of mine, Frank Down, had had an illustrious career. He was MD of Bewley's Cafés when I first met him, and he gave me my first job there. He had subsequently been promoted to business development director with the Campbell Bewley Group.

Then I heard through the grapevine that he had taken a Bewley's Café franchise, and I was confused. Why would a man with such a good job go back to running a café? It was only when I saw him sell the franchise to another Bewley's man, the former financial controller, Ian Conlon, and saw Frank take on the food franchise at Bewley's Hotel in Newlands Cross, that I realised that any move I made *towards* my goal of becoming a business owner did not have to be permanent – it could be just a stepping stone.

So I decided that I was willing to become self-employed for a time. I was willing to run my own café. It was vitally important to me, however, that this was only a stepping stone towards the right-hand side of the quadrant. Otherwise, I wouldn't have done it.

CHAPTER 4
Burning the Boats

Bewley's Franchising

In 1995, I was asked to take over Bewley's Franchising as GM. I was delighted.

I was delighted for a number of reasons. First, at age thirty-two, I would, for the first time, get weekends off! I had taken my first Saturday job in 1976, when I was thirteen, working as a trolley boy at the H Williams supermarket in Donaghmede Shopping Centre. So, for almost two decades, I had worked every Saturday. Second, in my new position, I would have a company car. The nature of the job meant that I would travel all around the country to visit, check on and support a plethora of cafés, and their owners. Finally, I had become tired in Bewley's on Grafton Street and was ready to move on. I believe we must remain fresh in our roles. I had contributed a lot to the evolution of Bewley's on Grafton Street, but I felt I had nothing more to give – it was time to pass the baton to the wonderful Deirdre Clarke, who went on to refresh the place for the next few years.

Bobby Kerr is a big man and a big personality. You may know him from RTÉ's *Dragons' Den* or as CEO of Insomnia Coffee Company. He had become MD of Bewley's Cafés around the time Frank Down went on to his role in the Campbell Bewley Group, and so he was my boss. But we started out on the wrong foot. An evening had been arranged for all the senior people to go out to eat and enjoy a few drinks to celebrate Bobby's appointment. I didn't go. Not that I didn't want to, but I was on holiday, and I was away when the date was changed for the night out, so I simply missed it. I heard Mr Kerr was a bit put out. Perhaps for that reason, or perhaps for others I am unaware of, there was an air of tension between us for a while. Until, one day, we went to Germany together on a business trip.

I admit I was not looking forward to it, but I put on a brave face. We arrived at our destination in Frankfurt and were hosted by an expat who had lived there for twenty years or so. When our tour of potential sites for a Bewley's operation was finished, Bobby and I went for some drinks. It was only then that things loosened up between us. From memory, we had a good heart-to-heart talk but, more importantly, we had great fun. My lasting memory of that trip is of us at 2 AM in some 'local', playing table football: Ireland vs. Germany, me and Bobby against two German guys. It was pure, harmless fun, but it broke the ice. Bobby and I have been friends since then. Bewley's never opened in Germany.

My role in Bewley's Franchising was an interesting one. It had three main parts: 1) policeman, protecting the brand; 2) liaison officer, acting as the link between the company and the business owners who had invested their money in our brand; and 3) development executive, vetting people and locations for future Bewley's franchises.

I thoroughly enjoyed the job, and learned a lot. I found that my many years of experience – particularly as GM of the flagship store on Grafton Street – gave me a unique perspective. But I found it difficult too: mainly because I was on my own. At the operation in Grafton Street, I had managed a team of twenty, who had managed a team of two hundred. Now it was just me with one support person, Carol, back in the office. I found that hard.

Bewley's Hotels

I looked at all the traffic and instantly I knew that the place was going to fly.

Standing in a field with Geraldine Allen, wife of Wexford beef baron and property tycoon Bert Allen, I could see the back of Bill Cullen's Renault showroom at Newlands Cross, on what back then was called the Naas dual carriageway. Geraldine was explaining to me their plans to build a hotel with an adjoining café/restaurant for which they wanted permission to use the Bewley's brand.

Immediately, I knew it would work. In fact, I believed it would work so well that, if Bewley's wasn't careful, it would lose out, big time. You see, Bewley's is the best-known Irish brand in Ireland, next to Guinness. So putting a Bewley's sign on the Naas Road at Newlands Cross was a no-brainer. The Allens knew that, and so did I.

By my reckoning, the whole campus would become known as Bewley's at Newlands Cross, regardless of what name was chosen for the hotel. So, following a cup of tea with Geraldine at the Green Isle Hotel up the road, I scooted back into town to meet my boss.

'That's a good idea,' Bobby Kerr said, as I explained to him why I believed we should only grant licence to use the Bewley's brand for the project if it was used on both the hotel and the café.

So Bobby took it to the board, and I stayed in touch with the Allens. A meeting was scheduled in a hotel room in the Glen of the Downs, which Bobby and I attended with Bert Allen and his lieutenant, Patsy Asple. We tabled the idea.

In fairness, the men were open to it. It had a certain ring to it, but there was no real precedent for the idea. There was, at the time, a poor excuse for a Bewley's Hotel above the Westmoreland Street café, but it certainly was not a model that could be easily replicated. It was higgledy-piggledy, to say the least. So this was new territory.

The Allens' management team was *not* excited. One even went so far as to say she thought the Bewley's brand would cheapen their offering but, in fairness to Bert Allen, when he sees an opportunity, he follows through. So a deal was struck. The Allens would build a hotel and a café on the site, and it would be known as Bewley's at Newlands Cross.

The fun began then, as we started to plan the restaurant. What style would it be? How would we retain the Bewley's atmosphere? What would happen at night? How would it become a restaurant as opposed to a café? Myriad questions we had no hope of answering definitively until we were trading. Trust and faith were required.

I was in the thick of it, as we drew heavily on the recent innovations we had put into the Bewley's Café in the Liffey Valley Shopping Centre, which I had helped to design, and which was the best-performing café on a revenue-per-seat-per-week basis that Bewley's had ever seen. And, two years after my meeting with Geraldine, we opened Bewley's at Newlands Cross. I personally served the first breakfast.

And it turns out that I was right – the project did fly!

Happy Birthday to Me

It was 30 March 1998, a Monday, and I was not happy. I had to travel to Tralee in County Kerry, which meant an overnight in Limerick on the way back, arriving at our home in Celbridge sometime on the Tuesday.

The reason I was not happy had nothing to do with Tralee or Limerick. It had to do with the fact that it was my birthday. And not just any birthday – my thirty-fifth! A birthday with a zero or a five has always held more significance for me, so to be away on my thirty-fifth just upset me. However, those forty-eight hours away changed my life forever.

I had tried to fob them off, I really had, but Donal O'Doherty and Colette Garvey were persistent. They wanted a Bewley's franchise for Tralee, but I had told them I didn't think it would work. I thought that was the end of it, but Colette didn't.

'I'm not accepting that from you as you sit in your office in Dublin,' she said. 'If you're going to say no, I want you down here in Tralee, having walked the land as you say it!'

Wow. I had met me match. So off I trooped.

To make sense of the trip, I booked into Jurys Inn in Limerick and arranged to meet a contact in Bewley's Café on Cruises Street the following morning at 8 AM just as it opened. I was then going to meet the Limerick Bewley's franchise owners, Des, Donald and Pat at 9.30 AM.

I arrived in Tralee around lunchtime and found it charming. Donal and Colette were equally charming, and we had a super time together. They took me on a walking tour of the town and showed me all the spots, including the location of the Dome for the annual Rose of Tralee International Festival. We really had a nice time.

Then Donal and Colette invited me to their home close to Tralee Bay. One thing is forever emblazoned on my memory from that visit: the magnificent view from their front door. The legendary Dingle Peninsula stretching off to my left appeared almost close enough to touch.

And it was at that moment that I got it. There was life beyond the Pale. The Pale, for those of you unfamiliar with it, is an historical term dating back to the fifteenth century. It denoted an imaginary line from Dalkey in south County Dublin to Dundalk, beyond which rural Ireland began. In the twenty-first century, the imaginary line of the Pale has been replaced by the M50.

Anyway, I saw it. It was real. People lived and worked, loved and laughed outside Dublin. Commerce happened, wealth was created and dreams came true or were shattered in Tralee as well as in Dublin. Why hadn't I seen it before? The realisation intrigued me. What would it be like living outside Dublin? In the 'country'?

I was treated to a birthday dinner by Donal and Colette in a nice, little first-floor Chinese restaurant and, as the evening progressed, with convivial conversation, I began to feel very much at home. They even arranged a candle on a slice of cake to mark the occasion. I was with new friends.

I still said no to their franchise request, though.

A Bad Start to a Good Day

Jurys Inn was basic enough, but it did the job. I had arrived tired from Kerry around 1 AM and grabbed a few hours of shut-eye before the start of my day in Limerick. I had been to Limerick many times before as franchise manager, so I knew my way around, and the Bewley's Café on Cruises Street was less than ten minutes' walk. The streets were very quiet as I strolled downtown at 7.45 AM. It was very different to Dublin, which would have been coming alive at that very time.

Try as I might, I cannot remember the purpose of my meeting with P.J. Power. Since he was an auctioneer in town, I assume it must have been to do with property. Anyway, he and I were meeting at Bewley's Café at 8 AM, and we arrived simultaneously from different directions. The door was opened by a staff member, and in we went. The effect on me was immediate and profound. I knew instantly that this was not going to be a quality Bewley's experience.

The place felt cold, and there was a definite lack of attention to detail. The breakfast cereal display lacked imagination. The fresh orange juices had clearly been poured the night before: the pulp had settled to the bottom of the few glasses that were available, and there were paper coffee coasters on top to keep dust from falling into the juice overnight. My overriding memory was of a less-than-average breakfast experience and, as protector of the brand, I was suitably embarrassed.

P.J. and I ate on our own for a long while before the next customers arrived and, as we spoke, it became clear from his comments that what we were experiencing was the norm. Bewley's in Limerick really wasn't a special experience. It was then that he said to me, 'If the right fella got his hands on this place, he could make a fortune.' A light bulb began to flicker in my head. I wondered if I could be that right fella.

After we finished our breakfast meeting and said goodbye, P.J. headed for his office uptown, and I stayed for my meeting with the franchise owners later in the morning.

Des, Donald and Pat were Limerick-based businessmen. They each owned independent businesses and also collaborated on a few. Each was hands-on in his own business and, as a result, had made a lot of money. They invested in other businesses that had potential, one of which was the Bewley's Café franchise at Cruises Street, which was suffering from lack of TLC. A series of managers had been appointed since it opened in 1992, but there was an obvious dearth of quality leadership and direction. Maybe P.J. Power had been right. If the right fella . . .

I was fresh from my 'beyond the Pale' experience of the previous day, having met wonderful people who earned a living and had a nice life in Tralee. I asked myself what life would be like if I gave it all up and moved to Limerick. How would we make it work? What would Aido and the kids think? I had no money. Did I really want to go back to working in a café, go back to working weekends and Christmases? Questions, questions, questions – and no answers.

Would You Buy the Place?

And that was where my head was at when a staff member woke me from my thoughts to tell me I had a phone call.

'For me?' I inquired. 'Who is it?'

'Des,' she said. 'The phone is in the kitchen.'

Des was the de facto spokesperson for the trio, so this was not unusual. What was unusual, however, was that he had called instead of appearing for our planned meeting. *Something must be wrong*, I thought.

I was led through the café which, by that time, was filling up – although the business level was nothing compared to Bewley's cafés in Dublin – and escorted behind the service counters, through a door and into a long, narrow kitchen.

At one end was a walk-in fridge. At the other was a doorway leading to a goods-inwards area. To the left as I looked towards the service doorway was a long bank of cooking equipment under a large stainless-steel extract canopy. To the right were a pastry-preparation area and a separate pot-wash sink station. Everything was clean and appropriately separated and segregated. Ovens were alive, pots were bubbling and the smell of scones baking was quite divine.

I grabbed the receiver from the wall phone.

'Hello.'

'Colm? Good morning. Desmond here. How are you?'

'Fine, thanks, Des how are you? Is everything OK?'

'Everything's fine thanks, but I'm afraid we're running late and won't get to you until much later. Can you hang around?'

'Hmmm. I'm afraid not, Des. I have to get back. Perhaps we can reschedule?'

'Yes, let's. And, once again, I'm sorry,' said Des.

It was only then that I noticed the kitchen was empty. I hadn't picked up on that before. I had passed the head chef, Josie, and the pastry chef, Bernie, as I walked in. They were serving breakfasts on the hot counter and filling the confectionery counter with delicious gateaux, fresh cream cakes and scones but, just at that moment, and very unusually, the kitchen was empty. It was just me on the phone to Des.

'I'm wondering, could I get involved down here?' I blurted out, unable to take back the words as they tumbled from my mouth.

There was a pause.

'What do you mean?' said Des.

'I have absolutely no idea,' I heard myself say. 'I just feel perhaps I could add some value here. I think I'm looking for opportunity.'

'Would you buy the place?' he asked.

'I have no money, but perhaps I could rent it?' I said sheepishly.

'Let's get together and have a chat. Come back on Saturday,' Des said.

I hung up. What had just happened? What can of worms had I opened? I was confused, but excitedly so. I had taken a bold first step and had no idea where it might lead.

The die was cast.

Limerick, You're a Lady

And so it was that I arrived home to Aido, Shóna and Steve on 31 March 1998 a changed man. I had turned thirty-five since I'd left two days earlier, and had asked the question that would change the course of our lives forever. But it felt right.

Aido was unsure, to say the least, and the next few days were a blur of questions asked and opinions of very little substance given. The only thing to do was to go back to Limerick for a visit.

So, early on the morning of the following Saturday, we left the kids with friends, and the two of us headed to Limerick. In pre-motorway Ireland, the journey seemed to last forever. But finally we arrived.

Cruises Street, in the heart of Limerick, is a pedestrian street. It was built on the site of the former Cruises Hotel, the source of the name, and was heralded as Limerick's answer to Grafton Street. The Bewley's Café was on Quimper Square, right at the heart of the street – at a pedestrian crossroads, so to speak. The square was constructed in such a way that it was, in fact, diamond-shaped as you approached. The café was clearly a landmark.

I parked strategically uptown, to allow Aido to get a feel for the city as we walked towards Cruises Street. It's fair to say that she was pleasantly surprised. She found herself facing a three-storey façade with a typical Bewley's-style mahogany entrance, well lit with faux-brass lamps, atop which were multiple window baskets marking the upstairs seating area. A few outside tables completed the scene.

'Let's say nothing and just have lunch,' I suggested, as I pulled the brass handle to open to door.

It was locked. I tried again. It didn't budge. I looked at my watch, and it was only 2 PM. No Bewley's Café should be closed at 2 PM on a Saturday. What was going on? We tried the other two doors; same story. By this time, we were completely thrown, so I began peering in through the large plate-glass windows to see what was happening. The place was devoid of custom, but there were a handful of staff milling around, so I knocked. Recognised by the assistant manager, Aideen O'Shaughnessy, we were admitted.

'A flood,' was her response to the obvious question. 'Our dishwasher overflowed.'

She led us towards the back of the long, narrow ground floor, past the breakfast counter, salad bar, hot counter, confectionery section and both coffee stations. True enough, the whole back section of the café was under an inch of sudsy water, which was emanating from under a doorway that led to the offending dishwasher. She had apparently called the plumber, who was en route, and the franchise owners, who had agreed to her shutting the shop.

I was taken aback. It was the busiest day of the week, and the place was closed. Regardless of the flood, 80 percent of the restaurant – including the fabulous upstairs seating area – remained unaffected. My immediate reaction was that, had I owned the business, the response would have been very different. The café would have remained open while the problem was contained and sorted.

Aido's initial good impression was shaken.

Money Is the Last Thing You Need

I don't remember feeling nervous as Aido and I walked into the Castletroy Park Hotel, a then five-star establishment set up by the legendary Chuck Feeney on the Dublin Road, close to the University of Limerick. Donald, Pat and Des were sitting in the conservatory, ready to meet with us. Introductions were made, coffee ordered and pleasantries exchanged. Aido hadn't met them before.

A more diverse group of people in consortium would be hard to find. Des – or Desmond, as he preferred to be called – was tall and heavily moustachioed. He spoke with a deep, cultured accent and was rarely seen without a cigar in mouth. He was known locally as a publican, and he oversaw with eagle eye a tremendous sports bar and restaurant complex called Punches. He had an infectious laugh, and his whole body would rock as he regaled us with stories and anecdotes.

Donald, a heavy set, tall man with prominent eyes and a Limerick accent, was quieter. He was a pharmacist, again with a renowned business in his field in the city. Pat was smaller and wirier, with bright eyes. He was also moustachioed and pushed his mouth to one side as he spoke. He was also a publican, but with a very different type of pub, in a different part of town. The three had known each other for years and had collaborated on at least two restaurant operations: Centre Piece Café in the Crescent Shopping Centre, Dooradoyle; and the Bewley's Café franchise on Cruises Street.

The week had been a blur. Monday, Tralee, Tuesday, Limerick, when Des had asked if we'd buy the place. This was Saturday. We had no money. I had no idea why we were sitting there.

In fairness to the three of them, all experienced businessmen, they were completely charming. They never once made us feel like the naïve business virgins we were deep down. The reality was, we had no clue and no plan. I just had a gut feeling, and Aido was willing to go along with me.

'What have you got in mind?' Des asked.

'I still don't know,' I replied.

I went on to say that I felt the time had come for Aido and I to do our own thing. I thought perhaps they would consider leasing or renting – I didn't even know if there was a difference – the business to us. With my many years of experience in the industry, generally, and in Bewley's, in particular, I felt I could add value to the operation, and that it would generate a positive financial return for us and them.

'Would you not buy it?' he asked again.

'With what?' I said. 'We have no money.'

'Money is the last thing you need,' was his astounding reply.

Then the three of them went into overdrive, working out how much the banks would lend based on the turnover and profitability of the business at that time, and how much cash flow could be generated in the first month of trade, given that we wouldn't have to pay our suppliers for thirty days. By the end of it, they had proposed that they would help us in any way they could, using their contacts and knowledge to get us access to as much institutional funding as possible and – here was the kicker – they would lend us any difference between what could be raised and the price we would pay for the business. Money *was* the last thing we needed!

Eight Short Weeks

Then began some of the most intense weeks of our lives, before or since.

We left Limerick to head back to Celbridge, our heads swimming with what had just happened. From nowhere, within a week we had a real opportunity to acquire our first business. But that's not quite true, is it? It wasn't really from nowhere.

You see, I had been grafting hard, very hard, to learn my trade for eighteen years. I had rarely missed a day's work. I had always tried to do the job right. I had run quality operations. I had operational knowledge (buckets of it), management knowledge (tons of it), corporate experience (in spades) and an intimate knowledge of the great brand, Bewley's. In all, I had more than forty thousand hours experience under my belt; it's generally agreed that it takes ten thousand hours to become a true professional in any field. It was the combination of all of that, which had led to the situation we found ourselves in – it couldn't have happened otherwise.

Had we agreed to buy the place before we left the Castletroy Park? I don't remember. Probably not. But we *had* agreed to take the next step towards that potential outcome. Was a price mentioned? No. The price would evolve from our deliberations in the coming weeks. And so the work began.

I rang Timo (Tim O'Keeffe), an old school friend who had become an accountant, and Mousey (Kevin Callan), a mate from The Grove who was a solicitor, to seek their advice. They were both great and guided us best they could.

The boys in Limerick arranged a meeting for us with their

bank, which happened to be in Cork, where Donald's brother, Pat Dempsey, was the branch manager. Donald and Des even came along with us. Pat interviewed us, this young couple with a family, and he liked what he saw. We had presence, obvious work ethic, ambition and experience. The business was performing well, with turnover of about £800,000 a year. It held the brand of a national institution. The boys, his clients, were willing to back us. We were bankable and the project was bankable. And so he said that yes, subject to the right deal being done, he would be happy to recommend us to the bank for approval.

All that remained was to agree a price with the three *amigos*. Interestingly, Donald, the quiet one, was put in charge of the negotiations. There were three elements to funding the deal:

1. A term loan based on a multiple of profits currently being generated in the business.

2. An overdraft based on the net cash flow expected in our first month of trade (income less current expenses such as wages and rent), which would start high and reduce from month to month until it reached an agreed level in an agreed period.

3. The gap between the sum of the term loan plus the overdraft, and what the boys wanted for the business. The boys had agreed to lend us the money to fill this gap.

The bank had agreed to points one and two, so we began to negotiate with the boys on point three. Soon a figure was agreed for the business, which, in turn, dictated the size of the gap; a rate of return was agreed for said gap funds. Deal done!

Eight short weeks from asking the question, we were headed for Limerick.

Limerick vs Perth

When I think back on it, it was mad really. From a standing start, with no money, within eight weeks we had virtually emigrated to another city and another life.

I found it particularly poignant that we drove to Dublin Airport en route to Limerick to wave my youngest sister Patricia and her husband, Paul Murphy, goodbye, as they headed to Perth, Australia for a year. I wasn't sure how to feel about that; they were going to the sun in Perth, and we were headed down the N7 to Limerick. Perth or Limerick, Limerick or Perth. Who was getting the better deal? In hindsight, both of us got good deals. I wondered, some years later, how that day was for Mam and Dad. In one fell swoop their nest became truly empty. Carol was in Perth already, and Ger and Donal were California. Mam and Dad were alone again, for the first time since 1962.

Aido and I arrived in Limerick on the June bank holiday weekend. It rained as we moved into our rented home in Dooradoyle. I understand it wasn't raining in Perth.

We knew nobody in Limerick. We knew very little about Limerick. We just moved for the opportunity that Bewley's Café on Cruises Street offered us as a family. So we had to start from scratch. Then, as now, the only thing to do was network. Very soon, we met a man called Michael, who was a former teacher turned property developer.

'I know of a rental in Dooradoyle,' says he.

'Where's that?' says I.

'Turn right at the Crescent Shopping Centre.'

'Where's that?'

'Oh, boy. Start on O'Connell Street and drive out of the city until you see McDonald's. Then take a left, and I'll be waiting in a purple RAV4 to take you the rest of the way.'

We really were clueless. Michael led us to the house, we settled in and then we headed to the café to finalise the deal. We still didn't own the place at that stage. We had agreed to buy it, but the paperwork was taking time. For a few weeks, we were effectively unemployed.

My mate Kevin Callan, the solicitor, had introduced me to his boss, Simon, and it was Simon who had worked with us on the finer points of the deal. He is a nice man and clearly had our interests at heart – but my God was it a painful process. I like to do stuff, not talk about it, and so I found the legal process very hard to deal with. Letters were exchanged back and forth between the sides, our people had incessant phone conversations with their people, and the only people making money were the legal eagles. Both sides were racking up expenses while Aido and I and the kids waited and waited and waited.

Eventually, I had enough. I called our guy, who was by then known to us as Simon the Sorcerer, and instructed him that we were done. Whilst we appreciated that he wanted a level of comfort around clause 15c of page thirty-nine of the intention to do blah, blah, blah, we needed to get on with it. And so we signed. Bewley's Café on Cruises Street was ours!

And it was still raining in Limerick, and still not raining in Perth.

The Burning of the Boats

Day one had arrived. We had the keys. We had the opportunity. We were finally in our own business, our fate clearly in our own hands. This was the big break: new city, new career phase – exciting times indeed. But, all of a sudden, it dawned on me. This was it. I was petrified! Metaphorically, we had burned the boats.

In 1519, a general by the name Hernán Cortés set sail from Cuba to the Yucatan, Mexico. Cortez, who had heard of the great riches of the Yucatan and had set his mind on conquering them, was in charge of eleven ships with more than five hundred soldiers, as well as one hundred sailors and sixteen horses. When Cortez and company finally arrived on shore, he suddenly turned to his men and ordered them to burn the boats. His soldiers' jaws dropped. Burn the boats? Then, how in the world would they get back? Cortez explained that they wouldn't *need* the boats, because they would conquer the Yucatan's armies and make their fortunes. And then they would take *the Yucatan's boats* home!

Think about it. We either had to make this thing work, or we were screwed. And all of a sudden, for the first time in this whirlwind adventure, I was scared stiff. Now, if you've been attentive so far, you'll notice that that is a trademark of mine. At almost every juncture, as my career changed, I was scared stiff. Big-time scared. By 1998, I knew that was my natural reaction to breaking out of my comfort zone, but I also knew by that the only way to expand my comfort zone *was* to break through.

Irrational thoughts flooded my brain. What if I can't do this? What if nobody comes through the doors? What if I'm not as good as I think I am? What if the staff members don't gel with me? What if there actually *is* a big secret and I missed it? What if? What if? What if? It was irrational, I know. I had been doing for my employers for almost two decades what I was now asking of myself. What was there to fear?

It's 8 AM on Monday, 22 June 1998, and I am about to open the doors of my very own café. I take a deep breath, turn the key and, to my great surprise, the first person through the door is one of my best friends in the world – John Barry, lovingly known to us all as J.B.

'What are you doing here?' I gasped.

'I couldn't *not* be your first customer,' he said. 'I came to wish you well.'

I was stunned. He had driven all the way from Dublin just to be our first customer. We hugged, and I offered him breakfast, which he accepted. Phew! I was off the hook. I didn't have to start just yet!

The two of us sat at the back of the café for an hour, batting back and forth about life and opportunity and the future and all sorts of stuff, J.B. beaming. Meanwhile, a growing, gnawing sense of dread welled up inside of me, building, building, building until, eventually, I said, 'J.B., I love you man, but I have to kick you out.'

The boats had been burned. There was only one way to the other side. J.B. left. I started.

CHAPTER 5
Sometimes I Win, and Sometimes I L . . .

Sometimes I win and Sometimes I L . . .

Did your mind automatically fill in the blank? Did it say 'lose'? Be honest – nobody's looking – most people say 'lose'.

Early on, when I began talking to Start Your Own Business groups on behalf of Bernadette Farrell and Ace Training, I would throw up a slide with 'Sometimes I win and sometimes I l . . .' and ask the audience to complete the sentence. Unanimously and in unison they would say 'lose' every time. So I began to expect it.

When I thought about it, it sort of made sense that these people, regardless of their ages or stages in life, who were stepping out on new phases in their personal journeys, publicly announcing that they thought they would like to start businesses, would assume that they would either win (the business would succeed) or lose (the business would fail). What threw me was that when I had the pleasure, on several occasions, of speaking to over one hundred seasoned business people and corporate types, they all said 'lose' too!

I then began to ask myself whether this was the result of a peculiarly Irish mindset – or perhaps a peculiarly European one? Our American cousins appear not to have this mentality. At least, the public American collective persona appears to shout success, not loss, most of the time.

But do you know what? I think it's at the very least a phenomenon of Western civilisation as a whole at the beginning of the twenty-first century. Maybe it's a function of our early years? Perhaps it's a derivative of those games we played as children or the sports we pursued in school where if you didn't win, well, you, er . . . lost.

But, of course, the more correct, infinitely more empowering version is, 'Sometimes I win and sometimes I *learn*.' Now, doesn't that feel better?

Imagine if you never lost again? How would that feel? Good, huh? Now please don't confuse this with winning every time, which, history teaches us, is impossible. But imagine if, every time you didn't win, you asked yourself what you could have done better, to give yourself a better chance of winning in similar circumstances next time.

As I was writing this, the British and Irish Lions had just won a three-test series in Australia, 2–1. The Lions won the first test 23–21, Australia won the second 16–15, and the Lions took the final test 41–16.

Look at what must've happened here. Australia didn't win the first test. They must have been upset, but they didn't throw their toys out of the pram, so to speak. They no doubt watched video from every angle, analysed the game frame by frame, play by play, and studied what and how they needed to improve if they were to win the second test. And they did! (Only just, mind you, but that's all it takes.) And what did the Lions do? Exactly the same as the Aussies had the week before when *they* didn't win – they learned.

Then they used that learning to improve and win the next time. And that's how they won the series.

Life by the Shannon

The reason I chose to open this section with a piece about learning rather than losing is that this is the sad part of the tale. This is where, despite my best intentions and fervent wishes, the universe decided to see what I was made of, and sent me numerous opportunities to prove my mettle.

Of course, it all started fine.

Once I kicked J.B. out and actually started to do what I had spent almost two decades practising, I remembered I was good at it. Indeed, as I said earlier, I was great at it. And I enjoyed it immensely.

Aido got involved from day one. She is a super manager, pernickety to a fault, and managed the money to a T. But she also discovered she had a talent for front-of-house operations and loved nothing more than spending a busy Saturday on the floor, managing and leading the team to deliver a service to the people of Limerick that at the time was second to none.

Life was good. Business was great.

Owning the franchise for Bewley's on Cruises Street really put us at the centre of things in the city. Cruises Street had struggled after opening in 1992. Initially lauded as the Grafton Street of Limerick, it had been dubbed 'Legoland' by an unimpressed press. But then it began to take off. National and multi-national brands saw its potential and, over time, it came into its own as a quality shopping and leisure area. It helped that it formed a conduit between the Milk Market, a traditional Saturday morning place of pilgrimage for city and country folk alike, and O'Connell

Street, Limerick's main thoroughfare. When we took over the Bewley's franchise, Cruises Street was on its upswing.

My training in – and love and understanding for – what the Bewley's brand was all about enabled us to provide a very credible Bewley's experience in Limerick. This, of course, was only possible because of some great management personnel and staff, most of whom we had inherited, all of whom we fell in love with. And business flew! In two years, the business increased by close to 30 percent.

As a family, we tried an au pair, but it was disastrous for us. We dropped that idea and, from then on, one or the other of us – mostly Aido, it has to be said – was at home with Shóna and Steve when they weren't in school. So we had a near-perfect balance.

Naturally a people person, I found myself becoming involved in Limerick life outside the walls of Bewley's Café. I had the great fortune of bumping into two guys early on who have been hugely influential and inspirational to me over the years. Pat O'Sullivan, the managing director of Masterchefs Hospitality and founder of the Café Noir chain, and another Pat, Slattery this time, former managing director of Advance Securities, now an international speaker and author. Through these two, I came into contact with literally hundreds of great people, many of whom I am still in contact with, or can reconnect with on foot of a phone call.

Your network is so important! Your income will always be the average of the incomes of five people you spend the most time with. Time for a change, perhaps?

Stand Up and Fight

I have to say, I *love* Limerick. The pride that Limerick people have in their wonderful city and county is palpable at times. It can be felt most when there is some major sporting event happening, such as a rugby match at Thomond Park Stadium.

Everybody in Limerick wears red in support of the provincial team, which is headquartered at Thomond Park. The men who wear the jersey for real are legends locally, but are as ordinary as the day is long. They are often seen in the city going about their normal lives and are respected enough to be left alone, bar the odd shout of support from across the street. But, in the early years, I didn't get it.

Aido was the first in our household to catch Red Fever. She was upset because every time there was a big Munster game on – whether at home, in another region or abroad – the café, our livelihood, would die for the day. So she decided to watch one of these games to see what all the hype was about. And that was it, Aido was *hooked*!

I was slower to catch on, and it was less the masterful rugby that eventually got me than the absolute pride these men in red drew from the entire population. And then it struck me: rugby in Limerick ignores social classification!

I'm a Dub. I attended St Paul's college in Raheny on Dublin's Northside, where rugby is *the* game. But I never played it, really. Oh, I tried, but it wasn't for me and, physically, I wasn't for it. But here's the thing. In Dublin, rugby has an air of elitism about it. I know this isn't true in all cases but, generally, rugby is perceived as a game for the middle and upper classes, the D4 set leading the charge with their support of the boys in blue, Munster's derby nemesis, Leinster.

In Limerick, it's in the blood. Everybody is involved, everybody is raised on it, and it is beautiful to witness. Let me give you one of my favourite examples of this all-encompassing allegiance to Munster rugby.

I was sitting in the waiting area of the Spotlight Stage School on O'Connell Street – a Limerick institution run, for more than a quarter of a century, by Judy O'Connor and Margaret Hough – about to collect Jenna, our youngest, one Saturday afternoon. I realised that most of the people there, young and old, were wearing red and there wasn't even a game on. The waiting area is like a wide hallway, with church-style pews lining the walls so that perhaps twelve people from all walks of life sit facing each other.

A small child, perhaps two years old, wearing his Munster kit, wanted out of his buggy. So his Munster-clad dad duly released him. And what would any self-respecting two-year-old do once the shackles were off? You're right; he ran straight down the hall between the pews while his dad launched into an immediate rugby-esque commentary about him 'making a break right up the middle, with the line clearly in his sights'. We all laughed. Both the dad and the child were thrilled.

I was blown away. This is real, people. And I love real.

The Munster motto is 'stand up and fight'. Little did I know that I would soon have to learn what that really means.

The Perfect Storm

You've probably seen the 2000 movie with George Clooney, but if not, let me summarise it for you here. *The Perfect Storm* tells the true story of a small fishing community in Gloucester, Massachusetts, devastated by the loss of a particular boat, the *Andrea Gail* and its crew of six men, on an ill-fated fishing trip to the Flemish Cap, an area of shallow waters in the North Atlantic Ocean, centred roughly 560 kilometres east of St John's, Newfoundland and Labrador. Despite warnings of bad weather on its proposed route, the *Andrea Gail* headed home to Gloucester from the Flemish Cap on 26 October 1991. Caught in nine-metre seas and 150-kilometre winds, Captain Frank W. 'Billy' Tyne Jr's last recorded words on 28 October were, 'She's comin' on, boys, and she's comin' on strong.'

This is a story about a captain and crew who were working hard, doing the thing they knew best, trying to earn a living, when a series of events beyond their control conspired against them and they lost their lives. May they rest in peace. Let's look at the events, which, individually, were not necessarily life-threatening, but in combination became fatal:

1. A 'nor'easter' absorbed Hurricane Grace – but this was hurricane season, so no biggie.

2. This storm was forced southward and became a cyclone. More dangerous, but still manageable.

3. It moved over warmer waters and became a tropical storm. Getting worse, but survivable.

4. It executed a loop and became a full-fledged hurricane again.

5. Captain Billy Tyne decided to go further out than originally planned – all the way to the Flemish Cap – because of a poor catch, a bad decision based on desperation.

6. The *Andrea Gail*'s ice machine malfunctioned so, despite the weather reports, Tyne decided to head for home so the Flemish Cap catch wouldn't spoil – a fatal decision because of all the other factors involved.

Remove any one of these separate incidents and perhaps the crew and the *Andrea Gail* would still be fishing today.

The analogy of the 'perfect storm' is useful for understanding what happened to us in the next stage of our lives. A whole series of events outside our control conspired to kill our café business. Despite the vast experience the team and I had, we were powerless to stop this process although, for a while, much like in the movie, we thought we were going to make it through.

In the end we didn't make it. We lost the café business. We lost €250,000. We nearly lost our home. We lost our confidence for a while. But there was no loss of life, thank God. And, as a result of the experience, when we dusted ourselves off and rose – somewhat battered and bruised – to start again, we were stronger for it.

Let me take you through our perfect storm.

Bacon, Egg and Sausage and Large Mugs of White Coffee

I love Bewley's, as you may have gathered by now. And one of the staple elements of the Bewley's café business over the years has been its world-famous breakfast. It is delicious. Not, perhaps, the healthiest fare on the planet, it must be said. Not the best thing to have every day of the week. But my goodness, it tastes great!

If you're Irish and of a certain, *ahem*, vintage, I bet you can taste it now. What's your favourite? Simple bacon, egg and sausage? With freshly baked brown bread? Scrambled eggs and bacon? Or, how about a white-pudding sandwich? You know what I'm talking about! And do you prefer tea or coffee with yours? For me, it was bacon, two eggs, sausage, hash browns, white pudding, white-bread toast and real butter. I'd go back for an extra slice of toast for the white-pudding sandwich as dessert, and wash it all down with a large mug of white coffee which, back in the day, was a delicious blend of one-third Bewley's Café Blend coffee and two-thirds steamed milk. Oh yeah! (Homer Simpson drool.)

We were operating our very own Bewley's franchise, and it was going well as the planet moved towards the dawn of a new millennium. Business was good, but we began to sense change in the air.

The bacon, egg and sausage and mugs of white coffee that Bewley's had, for 150 years, been famous for were being called into question by an ever more discerning, more widely travelled, more health-conscious emerging generation. It was happening slowly, almost imperceptibly, but happening nonetheless.

And then, all of a sudden, or so it seemed, people wanted sun-dried-tomato paninis instead of bacon butties, and lattes and cappuccinos instead of mugs of white coffee. A plethora of bespoke boutique coffee shops popped open like popping corn, offering said fare in modern settings. They attracted a whole swathe of customers from the emerging café generation. Bewley's, instead of becoming a classic, quickly became old.

Amusingly, I saw a great ad recently for a shopping centre in Dublin, boasting of its long history in this way: 'Established back when paninis were hang sangwiches.' *Hang sangwiches* is a colloquial term for ham sandwiches, most often consumed from tin-foil out of the boot of the car, alongside copious cups of *tae* (tea), by the side of the road, as legions of fans descended on Croke Park, the national stadium for Gaelic games such as hurling and Gaelic football.

Much like the *Titanic*, it takes a mammoth organisation and/or brand a long time to turn away from impending danger. It soon became obvious that there were going to be casualties. The brand and all of the individual Bewley's cafés – whether franchised or company-run – struggled to turn fast enough to a) offer the fare the public was clamouring for and b) become credibly associated with said new fare.

This was the first sign that a storm was brewing.

Dashboard Dining

So the tide was beginning to turn. The younger generation wanted stuff that their parents and grandparents couldn't have. They wanted modern. They wanted sexy. They wanted interesting. They wanted fast. They wanted convenient.

Bewley's, a classic again now in 2015, was, at the turn of the century, an old brand, representing the twentieth century. It was no longer cool. It was a place that the new generation's parents had dragged them to when they were kids. And, now that they were independent, they wanted none of it.

New and newly arrived coffee chains began to give the emerging coffee-drinking generation new flavours and tastes and exciting coffee-flavoured drinks. There was Perk (later Insomnia), founded and run by my friend and former boss Bobby Kerr. There was Mocha Beans, established by another former Bewley's colleague, Cathal Keogh. And Costa and Starbucks entered the Irish market. The young flocked to these new shops, and the market share of Bewley's diminished.

Then, to add fuel to the fire, we, as a nation, became busier. The Celtic tiger was a cub; the future looked bright. Fortune appeared to be favouring the bold, and so people began to work harder. Property prices were rising at staggering rates, but the Tiger Cub Generation wanted to get on the property ladder, and to do so meant moving farther and farther out from the cities' centres. A whole commuter-belt generation was created within ten years and, all of a sudden, people working in Dublin, for example, were commuting daily from towns such as Wicklow,

Carlow, Mullingar, Cavan, Navan and Drogheda.

The net result of this was that they were spending more time in the car, which meant less time at home and less time for 'frivolous' activities such as stopping for lunch or a coffee break. 'Time is money' was the ever-loudening mantra. They began seeing the necessity of feeding themselves as something that got in the way of earning money. The solution? Eating on the run. And so the once humble garage (petrol station) became a mecca for all things convenient.

Deli counters serving hot and cold foods were prolific. Excellent, fresh bean-to-cup coffee machines sprang up like nobody's business in the most backward former garages. Bewley's was among the brands that responded very well to this opportunity.

Savvy garage owners began to realise that, while you didn't *have to* stop to eat, you had to stop for fuel or you couldn't – er – make money. So, here was a perfect opportunity to offer both. While you were forced to stop for petrol, you could treat yourself to a latte and a panini to eat in traffic and, oh, by the way, how about some sweets for the kids? A newspaper perhaps? And what about flowers for your significant other, because you are going to be late home again?

People who once stopped for an hour for lunch no longer had that luxury. Many millions of euros of spending that once went to cafés and restaurants were now flooding into the cash registers in these garages, now reimagined as 'service stations'. Dashboard dining was flourishing.

This was the second element of our storm.

Foot-and-Mouth Disease

Foot-and-mouth disease, also known as hoof-and-mouth disease, affects cloven-hoofed animals, including sheep and cattle. It's highly infectious and sometimes fatal. Containing it involves vaccination, monitoring, trade restrictions and quarantines, and sometimes the elimination of millions of animals.

You might be thinking, Colm, thanks for the veterinary lesson, but what has this got to do with your café business failing? I'm getting to that. Patience.

You see, the third element facilitating the gathering storm was a foot-and-mouth disease (FMD) outbreak, Ireland's first in sixty years. It hit the UK first and, for three months, Ireland held its breath and made every effort to keep the disease from spreading across the sea; and then, when it did arrive, there were controls to limit its impact. These measures hit the tourism and service sectors hard, particularly in rural areas, because much of the countryside was placed off-limits for months. According to 'Impact of the 2001 Foot-and-Mouth Outbreak on the Irish Economy', a report by Ronnie O'Toole and Alan Matthews of Trinity College Dublin, and Michael Mulvey of Dublin Institute of Technology, 'the estimated negative impact on tourism revenues [was] €200 million'.

The bottom line was, people stopped moving. When people stop moving around, they can't spend. If they can't spend, we – the retailers and café operators – can't sell. If our sales are down, we require less staff, and fewer man-hours are employed. And so the vicious cycle continues. In that period in early to mid-2001, according to the report, rural areas were hurt the most. Limerick City isn't rural by any means, but it is situated in Ireland's Midwest, so a lot of its hinterland can be classified as rural. Many of Limerick's shoppers couldn't get to the city to shop.

To exacerbate matters, the outbreak early in the year, coupled with the government-imposed movement ban from March through May, played havoc with the summer travel plans of Irish residents. Some of those who may have been planning to holiday in Ireland decided to travel abroad, where it was 'safer'. Worst of all for centres such as Limerick, located adjacent to Shannon International Airport, the expected influx of foreign visitors that summer was severely impacted. In effect, there was a six-month period – including the whole summer – during which numbers of potential shoppers were significantly down.

Let's look at the storm brewing, shall we? Consumer tastes are changing, their commuting and eating habits are changing, more locations are offering food and beverages than ever before . . . and then everybody is effectively told to stay at home.

This is not good. Factor three enters our gathering storm.

9/11

Where were you when you heard?

I was in my office at Bewley's on Cruises Street in Limerick when a lovely man, Pat Mason, since deceased (RIP) rang me to ask if I had heard about a plane hitting one of the Twin Towers in New York. Of course, I hadn't heard and, like everybody else, I was stunned. I really couldn't take it all in. I rang home and Aido not only confirmed it but said it was all over the news and that a second plane had struck the second tower! I left the office and drove home in a daze and literally sat for the next few days, watching it over and over and over again, almost as though, if I watched it enough, it would turn out not to actually be real.

I was completely thrown by the sheer audacity and pure evil evident in such a callous attack on innocent civilians, and the realisation that, if the United States could be attacked like that in broad daylight, then there was no security anywhere anymore. I think I entered a brief period of depression, because I had no desire to move off the couch, no fight. Perhaps behind it all was a deep dread of what was going to happen to my business, which was already beginning to struggle after several profitable years.

The 9/11 attack could not have come at a worse time for us. It was devastating news for the Midwest, where, with Shannon International Airport just 'out the road', we were virtually always guaranteed an annual American tourist market before 9/11. Post 9/11, though, all bets were off.

With this fourth factor, the storm clouds were nearing critical mass.

1. Consumers' tastes had changed.

2. Their commuting and eating habits had changed. More locations were offering food than ever before, and coffee was no longer the preserve of a café environment; every 'garage' in the country had it.

3. For the previous six months, there has been no internal movement in Ireland, and no foreign visitors to the Midwest.

4. And now the Americans weren't coming back! They hadn't come in the summer of 2001 because of foot-and-mouth disease and now, because of the awful attacks on their very sovereignty, using – of all things – passenger airlines, they were not going to fly in 2002, either! There was going to be no early recovery for our fallen market.

Part of what affected me on that dreadful day, and for the days and weeks afterwards, was the realisation that our business might not survive this litany of complications.

And the problem was, we had burned the boats! There was no going back, only forward. We were nervous.

The Feckin' Celtic Tiger

'Feck' is an Irish-English (or, more correctly, Hiberno-English) variation on the obvious. It's not as harsh as its cousin.

Well, I want to tell you about the feckin' Celtic Tiger, using 'feck' to express my disbelief, pain, anger, not to mention contempt at the complete feck-up made of the Irish economy at the turn of the century, when vested interests, with assistance from a blind eye turned at the regulatory and governmental levels, allowed an unconscionable situation to arise. Basically, the 'paper value' of all Irish properties was rising and rising and rising, and it looked like it was never going to stop, so investors hiked up the rents on properties they owned, in line with said 'market values'.

I had never met the owners of our propery on Cruises Street. They were resident at that time, and perhaps still are, in Ballsbridge, D4. They sought a rent increase, as was their wont. As sole traders, we had in 1998 taken over a twenty-five-year lease which had commenced in 1992, with five-year upward-only rent reviews. At the time that we took it over, the rent, based on the market value of the property, was €146,000.

We could live with that. But, by 2002, the tenth anniversary of the establishment of the café on Cruises Street, the feckin' Celtic Tiger had caught the country by its tail, and everybody lost the run of themselves. The owners were seeking their second upward-only rent review, and were looking at telephone numbers as far as we were concerned. We objected. And, as is proper in these circumstances, our case went to arbitration in 2003.

The arbiter awarded the owners a rent of €313,000 per

annum, which worked out to €6,000 per week, or €1,000 per trading day! Rates added another €48,000 to the mix. So we faced a rent-and-rates bill of €361,000 per annum, virtually €1,000 for every day of the year! The madness brought on by the feckin' Celtic Tiger had not only sounded the death knell for our business but, in doing so, effectively killed Cruises Street by taking out its premier café.

Interestingly, we had received a call a year or so earlier from somebody offering €500,000 for the lease, which we had never followed up on. The reason: €500,000 would have been nothing once we'd cleared our debts on the business. And the café was our livelihood – what else were we going to do?

At time of writing 30 percent of premises on Cruises Street are vacant.

So, on top of declining sales brought on by a combination of consumer tastes changing, commuting and eating habits changing, more locations offering food, foot-and-mouth disease and the after-effects of 9/11, our rent increased by 114 percent.

Enter factor five. In our perfect storm, this was akin to the final thirty-foot wave that hit the *Andrea Gail*. We were fecked!

What Are We Going to Do Now?

It was quite a sobering time, as you can imagine.

Our sales were dropping. By 2003, they were back under €1 million a year. That's still a lot of revenue, but it isn't only how much you take in that matters; it is also how much you pay out and, ultimately, the difference between the two, that keeps you alive or kills you.

Let me tell you about our café's finances, using indicative values. If our gross sales was €1 million, and we paid about 20 percent of that in VAT, that left us with about €833,333 in net sales.

Here's where that money should have been going, more or less:

Budget Heading	Value (€)	% Net Sales	Comment
Net Sales	833,333	100	
Food Cost	250,000	30	
Labour Cost	250,000	30	
Rent and Rates	166,667	20	This is the figure a business like ours could afford. We were paying more than double.
Other Overheads	83,333	10	Industry standard
Profit	83,333	10	Fair expectation

Since we were being asked to pay €361,000 for rent and rates, this is what the picture actually looked like:

Budget Heading	Value (€)	% Net Sales	Comment
Net Sales	833,333	100	
Food Cost	250,000	30	
Labour Cost	250,000	30	
Rent and Rates	361,000	43	More than twice the standard
Other Overheads	83,333	10	Industry standard
Loss	(111,333)	(13)	Game over, unless you do something radical, quick!

Overnight, we had a problem – a big problem. One of the temptations in a difficult situation is to see it as hopeless and, like a rabbit in headlights, do nothing but sit there scared. The only thing I knew to do was to keep moving – hoping and praying all the while. Like Kiyosaki in his doomed helicopter, pushing *forward* on the joystick was the *last* thing I wanted to do, but I knew that doing nothing could be fatal. We had to do something, but what?

CHAPTER 6
The Man on the Train

2003

The year started off like most others. I had taken some time between Christmas and New Year's to review my life and set some goals for the year ahead, as is my habit. The rent arbitration I told you about in the last chapter hadn't happened yet, so I was living in glorious denial, thinking things were OK on the business front, and that we'd be fine.

The difference in 2003 was that we were turning forty! Aido is two weeks older than me – she'll kill me for telling you that – and so both of us were going to be forty in March 2003 #milestone. It needed celebrating, the question was how?

I remembered getting invited to a swathe of eighteenth birthday parties in own late teens, and I remembered thoroughly enjoying them. Then came the twenty-firsts, the twenty-fifths and the thirtieths – and now we and our peers were forty! How did that happen?

I began to think about those celebrations and they all, in my memory at least, had a common theme. They were all, in the main, held in some upstairs room in a bar, or at a local GAA club or similar such venue. The standard fluorescent lights were covered in film to reduce the glare, and the DJ was set up in the corner with alternating green, yellow and red lights. The more expensive DJs even brought portable disco balls. This was upmarket stuff, no messing here, ladies and gents.

And the food? It was always the same: a buffet prepared by an army of aunts and mothers, each of whom was charged with bringing their special dish. There was sliced ham, turkey, beef (at the fancier ones), bowls of salad, quartered tomatoes, coleslaw, potato salad, shop-bought bread rolls with foil-wrapped butter portions, apple tarts . . . and Aunty Mary's pavlova. Are you identifying with this? If you are an Irish child of the 60s or 70s, I expect you are.

Anyway, my problem was that they were all the same. Not that the eighteenths were all the same – that was to be expected. But the twenty-firsts were all the same as the eighteenths, and the twenty-fifths were the same as the twenty-firsts. And the thirtieths? Same. We had started to go to fortieths in our late thirties and, guess what, same, same. *Where's the growth here boys and girls?* I thought. *Where's the development? Surely heading to forty, life should have moved on somewhat?*

So I took a stand. There was no way we were celebrating our fortieths in the upstairs room of a pub with Aunty Mary's pavlova! But if we weren't going to do that, then what were we going to do instead? Because this was a milestone worth celebrating.

The answer came to me as I watched a Disney video with the kids. Let's go to Disneyland! So the five of us went to the Disney park in Florida for a week around Easter. We then went to the Gulf Coast for a further two weeks. Shóna was sixteen, Stephen was eight and Jenna was not yet two.

Then, in May, with a group of close friends, we hired Moy House, outside Lahinch, on the beautiful west coast of Clare, for a fabulous weekend. Moy House is a wonderful *Blue Book* bed and breakfast, complete with an 'honesty bar', where you helped yourself and noted in the book what you had drunk so that the establishment could charge you on your departure. (That worked well! I wonder if they have changed that policy.) Anyway, 2003 started well!

Build Something Significant!

I'm a reader. As a kid, I was something of a bookworm and would find myself getting lost in adventures such as *Treasure Island*. As a reader, the corresponding movie of a given book would often disappoint me, because the characters or setting looked wrong. I had imagined them differently and, in my opinion, often better.

In my teens, I was too cool to read, and I distinctly remember being in a Junior Cert exam and struggling with the spelling of a word for the first time in my life! I was shocked! I had never ever thought about spelling before and the reason was, I read. Copiously. And I loved it. Famous Five, Biggles and, in later years, UFO stories.

The first personal-development book I ever read was *Jonathon Livingston Seagull* by Richard Bach, and it blew my mind. I didn't know it was a personal-development book. I didn't even know personal development existed as a concept. A good friend, Elaine McCann, gave it to me for my twenty-first birthday. Believe it or not, I read it all in one sitting on the night of my twenty-first birthday party, which was held in a back room in the Portmarnock Country Club. I'm sure we had pavlova. I got home late, as you can imagine, and I was wired, so I started reading and I read and read and read until dawn. I was so fired up it wasn't funny! Having read the book cover to cover, I knew I wanted to do something. I was *bursting* to do something – I just didn't know what.

Fast forward to my fortieth. We stayed in the Wilderness Lodge hotel in Disney World in Florida, just 'coz. Far too expensive. But, hey, when were we going to be forty again? Never, that's right. From there, we took a rental home on Florida's Gulf Coast. The home was somebody's investment property and they obviously rented it out when they weren't using it. It had bits and pieces lying around, including books. Aido picked up a book and said, 'Col, you should read this.' I took it from her and worked out from the title, which escapes me now, that it was the story of seven giants of US industry, including Carnegie, Rockefeller, Morgan, Edison and Watson.

I read the book and, in it, one of these industrial giants, and I can't remember which, said, 'Build something significant!' And I thought, *That's it, that's what I want to do, I will build something significant.* The Merriam-Webster online dictionary gives 'significant' three definitions: 1) having meaning; 2a) having or likely to have influence; 2b) probably caused by something other than mere chance.

So I decided that, in my forties, I would strive to build a significant business. One that had meaning, was likely to have influence or effect and which would require effort, i.e. which would not happen by mere chance. Within a week of coming home from that wonderful celebration, I was on Dublin's Liffey Boardwalk with my brother Donal and a friend, Richard Styles, setting up the newly conceived Cruises Coffee Company kiosks.

This move would change my life, but not in the way I imagined.

Open Longer

Things had begun to tighten. Right through 2001, we knew that business was heading in the wrong direction, generally, and we knew there was an upwards-only rent review coming down the track in 2002, and so were looking for ways to increase business while at the same time maintaining or reducing other costs. When we looked at the resources available to us, we realised there were areas where we could make changes that could, perhaps, make a sufficient difference to keep the ship afloat. One was time: we could open earlier, later and on Sundays, if we so chose.

It's all very well opening longer and on more days in a week, but it only makes sense if there are potential customers available. Cruises Street was a shopping street, and it really worked only between 8 AM and 6 PM, Monday through Saturday, because that's when shoppers shop. So we had to look at when other groups of people were about and see if we could cater to them.

Sunday afternoon was an obvious one. There were always a few people – less, mind you, than before foot-and-mouth and before 9/11 – pottering around, looking for things to do and places to go on a Sunday. So we began to open Sundays. This helped a little, mainly because fixed costs such as rent, rates and bank loans were already theoretically paid between Monday and Saturday. But the change was not earth-shattering.

There were also the late-night revellers. Let me remind you here of the story I told earlier, whereby, back in my days as GM of Bewley's on Grafton Street, I remember leaving the building at 8 PM on a lovely summer evening after the café had closed – it used close at 7 PM, because we saw ourselves as operating on a shopping street – and realised that Grafton Street was thronged. When I spoke with Paddy Campbell, founder and chairman of the Campbell Bewley Group and said I believed we should stay open until 10 PM, he thought about it and said, 'Let's go to 1 AM!' This was a classic example of the difference in thinking between manager and owner, boys and girls. Anyway, we stayed open until 1 AM and it *rocked*! It was like turning on a fire hose. That extra late-night business was phenomenal. We ended up going until 3 AM and 4 AM to satisfy the 'let's have breakfast before we go to bed' brigade. Eventually, I believe, after I had moved on, the toll on the people and the premises and, perhaps, the brand, was too much. It was decided to pull it back in to a more-manageable 10 PM, which persists today.

So, I decided that perhaps there was a late-night opportunity in Cruises Street. The same street that, on a Saturday morning, was a conduit between the Milk Market and O'Connell Street was also the area where the busiest pubs and nightclubs were located and the city centre. It was worth a try. And try we did. Again, it helped a little, but not enough to warrant the extra costs and security it required, not to mention the toll on the people and the premises. So, after a period, we knocked it on the head.

But the ship was still leaking. If we didn't do something, it was going to sink. As you are no doubt aware from stories of ancient ships in peril, the captain and the sailors reputedly looked for stuff to dump overboard to stave off the danger, or at least delay the inevitable. It was time to look at ditching the Bewley's brand.

Cruises Coffee Co

Now, you already know how I feel about the Bewley's brand, so this was no easy decision. When I finally decided to step out on my own and become self-employed for the first time, despite my two decades of front-line experience, I chose to adopt an existing brand. The brand to me is all-important. It has to be bigger and have a life of its own beyond its founder and owners. Bewley's is that. The last thing I wanted to do was turn Bewley's in Cruises Street into Colm's Caf!

The fiscal reality, however, was that we were paying Bewley's about €50,000 per annum (5 percent of net revenue) for the use of the brand and its attendant systems, many of which I had contributed to creating and implementing. For me, this represented value for money, and I'd do it again tomorrow. It was just that our cafe – in that location, with that level of business, with an upwards-only rent review pending – simply couldn't afford it.

I had a meeting with Des Mahon, the franchise manager for Bewley's, to break the news. He understood. At the time, it was becoming apparent to Bewley's that they shouldn't really be in the franchise business, and it sort of suited them that we were cutting the umbilical. There was no animosity and every assistance was afforded. Mind you, we kept buying the coffee!

And so came the question of the brand. If it wasn't going to be Colm's Caf, then what? Again, we looked at our resources. Cruises Street. Coffee house. So why not Cruises Coffee Co?

I rang my graphic-design friend, who I had met through Bewley's back in the day. Simon Dry of Dry Design was the designer who had put the iconic diamond at the back of the slanted Bewley's logo, which was used for two decades and still adorns their HQ in Northern Cross, Dublin. For another client, Simon had also created the pink-and-purple pyramid for the Laser card. He and I had gotten on well, so I asked him to come up with a brand concept for Cruises Coffee Co. To help him along, I sent him an email with some photos and ideas.

Simon's early work, like any designer's, was squiggledy (good word). The idea was that after he had produced four or five concepts, we would choose one to develop.

Of the handful that he sent, which were all black-and-white, one jumped off the page. One of the photos I had sent him was of the statue outside the premises at Quimper Square on Cruises Street; the statue was of a traditional dancer from the French town Quimper, from which the name of the square was borrowed. In one of the designs, Simon used a representation of her shape as the 'i' in the word 'Cruises'. I loved it. At my request, we used blue and yellow as the colours.

Cruises Coffee Co was born. We rebranded the café at Cruises Street and, consequently, reinvigorated both our business and ourselves. We had something to fight for, and we had taken major steps towards taming our costs. Limerick people warmed to the new brand quickly.

Cruises on the Liffey

The Liffey, you may know, is the river that runs through – and divides – my birthplace, Dublin. When I was a child, it was smelly, immortalised by Bagatelle in their hit song, 'Summer in Dublin'. I'm a proud Northsider and, as such, the butt of many Southside jokes, such as, 'What do you call a Northsider in a suit? The defendant!' And, one of my favourites, 'What's the difference between a Northsider and Batman? Batman can actually go into town without robbin'!' You've got to be able to laugh at yourself.

My brothers, Ger and Donal, had been in California for close to a decade, and had carved out a music career for themselves there as The O'Brien Brothers. They had just arrived back in Ireland. Donal rang me to say that Dublin City Council had published a tender (public competition) seeking someone to operate the three coffee kiosks on the Liffey Boardwalk. Donal felt that he, I and a friend, Richard, should get together and bid. He had seen the success of small coffee kiosks in California and felt that perhaps the time had come in Ireland – ignoring the weather, of course. He then flew off to California again and left Richard and I to put together the tender document. We entered, and we got to interview stage.

Interestingly, on the day of our final interview, as we were walking along the boardwalks to our meeting, I realised why the kiosks – which at the time were being run by a company that shall remain nameless – weren't working so well. They were in the wrong places. Someone had decided to put each of the three coffee kiosks nearly in the centre of one of the three boardwalks.

To have a coffee, customers had to walk up to 250 metres east or west down a boardwalk, which limited the market to people already strolling on the boardwalks, and offered zero opportunity to attract the real foot traffic, which passed the ends of the boardwalks, going north or south.

When we got to our meeting, I boldly told the interviewer that, should we win, we would insist on the kiosks – which weighed several tons each – being moved as close as possible to the ends of the boardwalks, near the bridges spanning the Liffey. I explained the logic of 'location, location, location', and I said that, if City Council was not prepared to move the kiosks, they could count us out of the competition!

We won. The Council moved the kiosks, and they were ours to run. Which is why I found myself on the Liffey Boardwalks a week after my celebration in Florida with my family.

The original Cruises Coffee Co outlet in Limerick – formerly Bewley's – was trading well, and transferring the brand to Dublin wasn't a problem. People there didn't necessarily know that it was Limerick-born, since the name was generic, not parochial. My attitude has always been that there's no reason a global brand can't start from Limerick. Why must it always be Silicon Valley or Seattle? I began to imagine a coffee brand to rival the best and could see in my mind's eye a franchise opportunity alongside retail sales of coffee beans and ancillary products. We even designed the cups and the packaging. This was going to be huge!

The Cruises Coffee kiosks opened. The sun shone. The *craic* was mighty (we had great fun). Business was great.

This, I believed, was the start of me building something significant! Happy days.

The Man on the Train

'What does this mean?' he asked.

'What?' says I.

'This. Here on your business card. It says, "How can I help?" What does that mean?'

'Oh that? That'll mean something different to everybody I meet. It's my offer to the universe. You might need a ladder some-day, or an electrician – or anything. And perhaps you'll call me. If I can help, I will; if I can't, I might know of someone who can. Simple.'

'OK,' he said. He smiled as he pocketed my business card.

I hate driving! For me, it's a waste of time, except when you choose to use the time wisely by using CDs to study, instead of listening to the radio, which can often be negative because nega-tive sells. And it was precisely because I hate driving that I was on the train from Limerick to Dublin that fateful morning.

I was en route to meet Donal and Richard at the Cruises Coffee kiosks on the boardwalk. Taking the train from Limerick to Heuston Station and then a bus down the quays was the sim-plest option, and also the one I preferred. On the train, I could think, drink coffee, work on my laptop, read, drink coffee, snooze, drink coffee, think . . . you getting the picture?

As fate would have it, I sat beside this man, both of us facing forward: he by the window, me by the aisle. I can't remember whether I had pre-booked the seat or whether I simply sat down. However, we exchanged pleasantries and got on with our respec-tive train-journey stuff. At some point, we got chatting and it became appropriate to swap business cards, as is protocol when two people engaged in the economy meet. He was an O'Brien too, which was a good start. Gary O'Brien was working with PAUL Partnership, a not-for-profit organisation working to bridge the divide between society, in general, and areas of disad-vantage in Limerick.

I was back from Florida. Our new brand was beginning to grow legs. The rent arbitration was still some time away. It looked like we might make it, and so it was precisely because I was feeling rather blessed with prospective opportunity that the offer to the universe was on my card. But it was also that very offer to the universe, coupled with that very fateful meeting, which had created the thread that led to the lifeline that led me to the school-lunch business, which led to me sitting in a café overlooking the Mediterranean Sea ten years later and writing this chapter. This stuff must work.

Gary and I parted ways at Heuston Station. Three months later, his boss rang me.

'You met a man on the train,' he began. 'He has left PAUL Partnership, but he left me your card. I see you're in the food business. Are you interested in tendering for a healthy-school-lunch pilot project in a school in Moyross?'

Am I what? Er . . . yeah! I thought. The Limerick café business was dying, and I was desperate for an escape route. But I was cool and responded, 'Yes. We could probably look at something like that.'

Twenty-seven Lunches

And that was that. We won the tender. That was the tenuous link that led to what has become Carambola Kidz, a company with €5 million in annual turnover, employing over eighty people, working with ten partners, collectively creating jobs for 150 people in Ireland in 2014.

By the way, it turns out we were the only ones who tendered! I'd love to say that nobody else saw the opportunity but, in reality, I think nobody else was quite as desperate as we were.

Was that a good meeting? As they say in Limerick, 'You can chalk it down!' That was a *great* meeting! Oh, and by the way, there's one for everybody in the audience. (That's a catchphrase from the *Late Late Show*, an Irish institution.) Yes. There's one of those meetings for you too. If you are out there, working hard to make it happen, being open and positive and generous in spirit, my belief is your man-on-the-train moment will happen.

Here's a question with only one answer. Would the man on the train *ever* have knocked on my door and said, 'Sorry to interrupt you watching telly, but I have an opportunity for you to consider'? Answer: *no*! OK. We're on the same page, you and I? We agree we've got to be out there? Good.

Did I realise we had this opportunity on day one? No way. Our mission today is to help promote healthy-lifestyle awareness in all children; our mission in 2003 was to pay the rent! And so we began supplying Corpus Christi National School in Moyross, a notoriously disadvantaged area on the north side of Limerick. Our order for day one in late 2003 was for twenty-seven lunches.

Frankly, it was a pain in the neck. Far from being the thing that would save the café, it very quickly turned into an operational nightmare.

We were clueless. In an earlier section, I wrote that anything worth doing is worth doing badly until you learn to do it well. That was certainly the case with our school-lunch business. The only direction we were given was that we had to provide three items: a sandwich, a piece of fresh fruit and a drink. So, with my catering head on, I priced this feast at €1.99 per child per day.

As I said earlier, even though this price point won us the business, it was a mistake. I learned later that the government was funding the programme to the tune of only €1.20 per child per day – and that the difference between that and our price had to come from parents. And you will remember that the parents of the children who needed the programme the most couldn't or wouldn't put their hands in their pockets to cover the difference. So less than 10 percent of the school signed up.

We used take daily orders, which meant that each teacher had to fax us Little Johnny's order every day. Twenty-two faxes a day – one from each classroom – each with one or a handful of orders, had to be analysed, converted into an order for ingredients and then converted into a production list. This was a nightmare for our staff and a nightmare for the teachers, who wanted to focus on teaching, not acting as waiters and waitresses for seven-year-olds.

I was beginning to regret meeting the man on the train. In fact, it was so difficult that I nearly threw in the towel. Thank God I didn't.

Meanwhile . . . Back at the Ranch

And all this was going on against the backdrop of us trying to revive the flagging café business in Limerick, through the rebrand to Cruises Coffee Co.

We had opened a Cruises Coffee kiosk at Homebase on the Dublin Road in Limerick, and the kiosks in Dublin were going well. At least, they were trading well; we weren't making any money, but we weren't losing any either. We were busy people.

To me, my significant business was going to be Cruises Coffee Co. The café industry was where I had spent over two decades learning my trade, and so it was the most obvious choice. Therefore, that's where I spent most of my time.

To help my main café business along, I met Limerick City Coordinator Andrew Mawhinny, and we called a meeting of city-centre traders, thinking a rising tide lifts all boats so we should band together to promote city-centre business. The invitation we sent out through the Limerick Chamber of Commerce had the strapline 'They Is You!' It was a phrase I picked up from one of Zig Ziglar's books, meaning that the famous committee of 'they' is made up of you and me. If you find yourself saying, 'They should . . .' or, 'If only they would . . .' well, really you're talking about yourself.

We even invited the mayor to the meeting, which was called for 1 PM in a large room that could be sectioned off at the front of Cruises Café. It was a sign of how bad things were that we could afford to cordon off such a space at lunchtime.

At 1 PM, the only people there were Andrew and I! Had we

misread the sentiment on the streets? We were convinced that the city centre was struggling, and not just Cruises Café. Had the message on the invitation been too strong? Too cryptic? We even had food laid on!

Then, at about three minutes past the hour, the proverbial floodgates opened, as a line of Limerick's good and great formed at the entrance to the room, snaking through the café and down the stairs. By 1.10 PM, there were seventy retailers and Chamber members in the room with the mayor. Turns out we had nailed the mood in the city.

To be honest, I don't remember exactly who said what that day. I'm sure Andrew opened the proceedings, and I know the mayor said a few words. I thanked everyone for coming and said that I, for one, was willing to put my hand in the air and state that I was finding business tough and that, if others felt the same, maybe we should stop competing and work together to get more business into the city – if it worked, we would all share in the rewards. Most agreed. The speeches ended, the buffet opened and people networked and chatted.

It was a success as an event, the question was, what were we going to do as a result? The answer: we founded the Limerick City Business Association (LCBA) and began to work together towards a better retail-business environment in the city. More than ten years on, the LCBA has been subsumed into the Limerick Chamber as a separate division representing the voice of city-centre retailers. That meeting is still paying dividends.

The Writing on the Wall

I had seen a lovely stencil job done at Bewley's Café on Westmoreland Street, where individual words and phrases were applied to a painted wall. It was very eye-catching and interesting, so, when we rebranded to Cruises, as part of the makeover, I asked Tony Murphy, of United Colours, to provide us with something like it. He did an outstanding job. I was unaware how difficult large-scale stencilling is, but, to Tony's credit, he stuck at it, and the result was one that he and I were both proud of.

The Cruises Café colours differed from the Bewley's colours. Bewley's used burgundy and black, and Cruises used blue and yellow for a brighter, more modern feel. I was very happy with how the café – which was physically the same structure and still used the same furniture – lent itself to the new, brighter colours. It worked.

However there was writing on the wall of a different, far more dangerous type than Tony's stencilling. It came in the form of the arbitration decision awarding our landlords €313,000 a year for the next five years. This writing, once decoded, translated into 'it's over!'

We had hit the iceberg. The *Titanic* was going to sink. There was no way a café of our size, at our location, at that time, with the menu we offered, at the price points and margins we operated at, would survive that blow. We had to move from a rescue operation to a recovery operation overnight. Two questions loomed: 1) how long did we have? 2) What could we salvage?

We were now *haemorrhaging* money. Every day we woke up there was, effectively, another €1,000 bill for rent lying on the mat. We still had staff and suppliers to pay and lights to keep lit – all the usual stuff – while we searched frantically for solutions. We painted on smiles and pursued two avenues. One was a search for a business model that could work given the café's size, location and rent. The other was a search for a buyer for the lease, to get this noose off of our necks.

On the business-model front, a convenience store was mooted and I pursued it vigorously. Based on a meeting with Spar, who are experts in the field, it looked like we could probably turn over €90,000 a week, which was huge, but that the margins would be extremely tight, so the rent still made the opportunity marginal, at best.

Despite our best efforts, we couldn't find anybody with the appetite to fund the transformation from café to convenience store. So that avenue closed. However, as fate would have it, I met an accountant while looking for a potential suitor for Spar on Cruises Street, and that accountant, Ger Dillon is now a co-director and partner in Carambola Kidz. Sometimes I win and sometimes I . . .

Simultaneously, we put the lease up for sale – quietly, so as not to disconcert our customers, staff and suppliers. After another year, and another €313,000 in rent, we finally got a nibble. The UK fashion chain New Look expressed interest. We needed to hook them, and fast!

That'll Be Seventy-five Grand, Thanks

We were working against the clock big-time by now. Every day that we remained in control of the lease was a day we were getting further into the red. New Look had been brought to us by real estate broker Lisney, and they felt they could get a deal over the line if the price was right.

We were heading rapidly towards €425,000 in debt, so that was our ideal exit figure, but we had run out of runway to allow for negotiation. So we sought advice as to how much New Look would pay for the opportunity to control the lease on Cruises Street, and the figure that came back was €250,000. This meant we would be virtually unemployed, with a business debt of €175,000! However, at least the hole wouldn't be getting any deeper. So we said yes, we would exit for €250,000.

Then, just when you think it's safe to go back in the water, due diligence kicks in. Their suits need to talk with ours, emails need sending, opinions need forming, facts need verifying and on and on and on and, in the meantime, the €1,000-per-day clock was ticking. It was *vital* that this deal be done by Christmas 2004 so we could draw a line in the sand and regroup from 1 January 2005.

We all worked our tails off towards that very important deadline, while also maintaining the kiosks at Homebase and in Dublin, as well as the school-lunch thingy. I also chose to stay on at the LCBA, as it gave me access to positive people with a can-do attitude.

I told you earlier how Michael O'Leary had influenced my

decision-making around the school lunches. I believed he would trade margin for volume, and so I dropped our price from €1.99 per child per day to €1.20 – the price the government was paying – by mutual agreement with the principal of the one school we were serving and, in return, we got to feed all the children there. Our business rose more than tenfold overnight – still nowhere enough to get excited about, but a step in the right direction.

Much more importantly, PAUL Partnership was then able to take the model we had created to other disadvantaged schools in Limerick. Quite quickly, we were in nine schools and serving about 1,500 children. I finally began to take it seriously. This was certainly something we had to salvage from the *Titanic*, so we rented premises for it in Raheen Business Park. My dad came with me to Cork, and we opened up a new route there from September 2004. I did the deliveries there each morning.

Heading towards Christmas 2004, a game plan was unfolding. We would remortgage our home to raise €100,000 towards the €175,000 we believed would be left outstanding. We did a deal with our bankers to convert our overdraft (officially €30,000, but running at €80,000) into a term loan when the café closed. It'd be tough, but we believed we could handle it. And at least the bleeding would have stopped.

And then the unthinkable happened. We missed the Christmas deadline! We would need to pony up a further €78,500 in rent for the first quarter of 2005! My Mam and Dad came to the rescue by guaranteeing a loan of €75,000, for which we are very grateful, and which is close to being cleared as I write. We finally exited the premises on 4 March 2005, physically and emotionally exhausted, battered and bruised, carrying personal business-related debt in excess of €250,000.

CHAPTER 7
Breakthrough

The Trouble with Optimism

Admiral Jim Stockdale was the highest-ranking US Naval Officer imprisoned during the Vietnam War. He was in prison for seven and a half years and was tortured more than twenty times. He survived.

Stockdale's plane was hit by enemy fire over North Vietnam in 1965. He ejected and landed in a village. He was beaten, captured and held as a prisoner of war. As the senior naval officer in the Hoa Lo prison, he was one of the main organisers of resistance. When told, at one point, that he was to be paraded in public, he slit his scalp to disfigure himself so he couldn't be used for propaganda. His captors covered these wounds with a hat, so he beat himself in the face with a stool. At another point, he slit his own wrists so he couldn't be tortured into confessing sensitive information.

This guy was tough!

When author Jim Collins interviewed him for, of all things, a book about business (*Good to Great*), Stockdale gave two answers that really spoke to me.

Collins: 'How did you cope?'

Stockdale: 'I never lost faith in the end of the story, I never doubted not only that I would get out, but also that I would prevail in the end and turn the experience into the defining event of my life, which, in retrospect, I would not trade.'

Collins: 'Who didn't survive?'

Stockdale: 'Oh, that's easy, the optimists. Oh, they were the ones who said, "We're going to be out by Christmas." And

Christmas would come, and Christmas would go. Then they'd say, "We're going to be out by Easter." And Easter would come, and Easter would go. And then Thanksgiving, and then it would be Christmas again. And they died of a broken heart.'

When I read this answer, I was dumbounded. I had to read and reread it to fully grasp what this real-life hero was saying. He was effectively saying that the optimists amongst us, the people who see the best in situations – up to that point I had counted myself among these – might have it wrong!

Thankfully, Admiral Stockdale went on to clarify.

'This is a very important lesson,' he said. 'You must never confuse faith that you will prevail in the end – which you can never afford to lose – with the discipline to confront the most brutal facts of your current reality, whatever they might be.'

In other words, an inclination to put the most favourable construction upon actions and events or to anticipate the best possible outcome, isn't enough; it's a start – and a very good one – but it must be backed up by 'the discipline to confront the most brutal facts of your current reality'.

Our café had just failed spectacularly. We had no income. We owed €250,000. We had nearly lost our home. We had a long road ahead. But somehow, deep down, I was sure we'd survive and thrive.

You *Will* Get Paid, Trust Me

'There is no money. The café will close soon. I need you to trust me. I need you to continue supplying the café and also to contin-ue supplying the school-lunch business. You *will* get paid, I just can't say when.'

This was the gist of the conversation I started having with each of our suppliers in January 2005. It was not an easy one to have.

I was effectively asking each of them to a) not expect money for invoices that were coming due or were, perhaps, outstanding in January 2005, and b) to continue to supply both my business-es on credit and trust until further notice. To have them discon-tinue supply for any element of either business would have made it very difficult to continue trading. And we needed to continue trading to give ourselves a chance at surviving. We were treading very deep water and, if we stopped treading, we would drown. If one supplier cut us off, we would never find a replacement.

It was a lot to ask anybody. Imagine if you were a supplier to one or both businesses. (Initially, all of the suppliers to our school-lunch business were suppliers to our café business.) What would be your gut reaction to my request? Would you be nerv-ous? I would. Angry? Perhaps.

Effectively, we had three types of suppliers: corporates, SMEs and small mom-and-pop-style operations. Each one had its own unique process to go through to see whether they could or would support us. The mom-and-pops, at one level, were easiest; in most cases, we were dealing daily with the owner. However, being, in the main, the smallest operations, they had shallow pockets, so they couldn't help with our cash flow problem for an extended period.

SMEs are typically that bit bigger, with a management structure involving the guys on the ground (the salesmen, with whom we had the relationships) as well as the owners. The conversations started with the salesmen and very quickly entered the phase where the owners hurried in for meetings. In a funny sort of way, SMEs often have less access to funds than mom-and-pops. They are often highly indebted as a result of their investments in growing from mom-and-pop operations to become SMEs.

The corporates were a different animal altogether. Again, we dealt with the salesmen. But they would wheel in regional or perhaps national sales directors, who then had to put our case forward to their boards, with a recommendation. There was stress at all levels. The salesmen were in the spotlight for 'not seeing' this thing coming down the track; the directors, similarly, for not being on top of their sales people and their accounts.

But we found ourselves where we found ourselves, and no amount of 'if onlys' were going to make it go away. We all had to 'confront the most brutal facts of our current reality'. They all agreed! They agreed because of our track record. Every supplier continued supplying one or both businesses until we finally exited Cruises Street in March 2005. Once the dust settled, and we knew what funds we had access to, we met with each and closed off each account to the full satisfaction of all parties.

Looking for a Job Again

Naturally, one of the options I explored to salvage our personal situation was entering the job market again.

Aido and I reviewed our situation. It was bleak.

We had a mountain of debt. We were physically and emotionally exhausted. Cruises Coffee's kiosks were trading at breakeven: staff and suppliers were being paid, but there was no money for us. The school-lunch thingy had grown to perhaps 3,000 lunches per day, as a result of me buying the Merc and driving to Cork and back every day to do deliveries. Neither business looked like it would take off at sufficient pace to allow us get back to paying ourselves anytime soon.

The most obvious solution appeared to be to find someone who was interested in my talents and willing to write me a monthly pay cheque. I have to admit, attractive though this seemed – and in fairness this option had Aido's vote! – it signified failure to me. This was not my preferred option by a long shot, but needs must.

As fate would have it, I met a man, Kieran Walshe, who at the time controlled the company that owned the BB's Coffee & Muffins franchise for Ireland and the UK. Kieran is a very nice man as well as being a shrewd, savvy businessman. He and I hit it off. He began to talk to me of his plans for the BB's brand in Ireland, and we began to explore an option where, later in 2005, I would come on board as franchise manager to help develop existing stores and locate premises around the country into which BB's could expand. It seemed like a natural fit.

Starting in late 2005, whilst not ideal – Aido and I would have preferred that I start sooner – was better than nothing. Finally, it looked like there was light at the end of the tunnel, and it wasn't a train speeding towards us.

While we were waiting for Kieran to line things up in his organisation so that the role could be created, we kept on doing the things that needed doing to stay alive. Every morning, very early, I would load the van and drive to Cork to do our lunch deliveries, and then come back to the 'factory' in Raheen to begin preparing lunches for the following day. We still had legal and financial tangles that needed sorting, so that took a lot of time on weekday afternoons. And then, at the weekend, we had the kiosks to look after. We were as busy as ever. In the meantime, Kieran and I kept in contact.

I don't know what it was but, gradually, something entered the conversations with Kieran that gave me the 'feeling' that perhaps this much-talked-about and much-needed – from our perspective – job might not materialise. You know, when your intuition kicks in? You can't quite put your finger on it, but you know something has changed. I kept the feeling to myself for a while, because I knew Aido had her hopes set on it; prior to meeting me, she never had any ambition to be in business anyway.

Finally, I told her that I didn't think it would happen. I decided to 'get stuck in' to the lunch thingy to see what I could do.

Getting Stuck In

According to the dictionary, 'get stuck in' is an informal expression meaning 'to start doing something enthusiastically'.

I looked it up as I began writing this section. I was curious to know if there was an official definition for this figure of speech, which we use in such a blasé fashion. I was pleasantly surprised when the oracle that is Google presented me with the above definition from Cambridge Dictionaries.

It was time that I started doing the school-lunch thingy enthusiastically.

I had realised three things about it. First, that if Dad and I had managed to get extra business by hopping in a car and driving to another city, then perhaps there were more DEIS schools out there that would welcome our service. Second, by now we knew what we were doing and had the bones of a system that would allow us take on new business in a relatively simple way. Third, unlike our café, which had been dependent mainly on how many people passed its door, our 'factory' could supply customers anywhere. We could travel to find customers, rather than sitting there bemoaning the fact that they hadn't found us.

Anyway, I had nothing to lose, so I got stuck in. I got stuck in with gusto. And, in getting stuck in, I found my own definition for what that phrase means.

Ask me now what I did, exactly, and the answer would be simply everything. Did I make sandwiches? Yes. Pack lunches? Yes. Drive vans? Yes. Place orders? Yes. Visit schools? Yes. Make sales calls? Yes. Do deliveries? Yes. Pay bills? Yes. Mediate in staff rows? Yes. Stand on top of the recycling bin to compact the cardboard so I could squeeze in some more? Yes. Fix plugs? Yes. Wash out trays? Yes. Clean the toilets? Yes. Sleep? Not much.

Getting stuck in, in my opinion, is more than starting to do things enthusiastically. It is doing whatever it takes – for as long as it takes – to make something happen.

Now here's a challenge. One of the biggest problems with getting stuck in is the risk of getting sucked in to both the work and its attendant adrenalin, and to believing that it's all you. Also, if you're not careful, all of a sudden your very sense of self is derived from being the guy or the girl who makes it happen 24-7-365.

In my opinion, both of these side effects are dangerous, because they lead to burnout. Millions of self-employed people around the world hate the jobs they have created for themselves, doing work they once adored, because they got stuck in with no plan for how to replace themselves. This is a fundamental difference between the mentality of the self-employed person and the business owner. I never wanted to be self-employed (but was willing to be, for a time). I wanted to create a system into which I could draw others, who would eventually do the work.

From day one, I was planning to replace myself entirely. Today, I refuse to answer the phone in the office because if I do it means someone, whose job it is to answer the phone, isn't doing theirs.

A Typical Day in the Early Years (Morning)

4.30 AM: Beep, beep, beep, beep . . . alarm goes off. Time to get up. Jump into my jeans and work boots, pull on a sweatshirt, fill a flask with coffee and I'm out the door. It's –5° Celsius. Our estate is eerily quiet. There isn't a sound until I start up the Merc's 2.5-litre diesel engine. One sure way of getting a bad name with the neighbours is running a diesel engine to defrost the windscreen of a second-hand van so you can drive to work in the middle of the night. Thankfully, I remembered to put old sheets on the windscreen under the wipers last night; it's easier to peel them off, stiff and crystalline, than to try scraping the ice off. But the engine still has to be run to get the screen clear.

5 AM: Arrive at Raheen and begin the process of loading up. One thousand seven hundred lunches, at an average of twenty lunches per tray, is eighty-five trays. Each tray weighs about twenty kilograms, so I'll get a full work-out by 5.45 am. I take eight trays at a time on a hand cart and run them through the kitchen, down a ramp, to the back door of the van. I load each by hand (known in the trade as 'hand-balling') into the refrigerated compartment, climb in, re-stack them, and shuffle the stack into exact position for safe transport. Then I climb down and repeat the process ten more times. I'm sweating, despite the cold. Before I leave for Cork, I review orders for the following day to make sure the sandwich-makers, who will be in before I get back, have proper instructions.

6 AM to 8 AM: I load up my favourite motivational CDs and off

I go on the 250-kilometre round trip, watching the sun rise slowly as I travel. Two hours to myself. Bliss.

8 AM to 10.30 AM: Systems and rhythm are everything. I must be finished deliveries to all schools by 10.30 AM, before *sos beag* (little break), so taking account of where the schools were located, how many trays I have to deliver to each school, caretakers' habits – some were early risers, others were not – and traffic movements, I must be at my first school by 8 AM. Any delay will cause me problems. Johnny must be fed.

Every school is different. Some have steps to negotiate. At some, I can reverse to the front door. At others, I have to park on the street and 'hand-ball' the trays one hundred metres or more on my trusty handcart.

The trays for the first school on the route have been packed into the van last, so they are facing me when I arrive at 8 AM. The air temperature has warmed up to freezing by now.

As I deliver today's lunches, I collect yesterday's empty trays. These need stacking and shuffling so as not to impede my second, third and subsequent deliveries. This is work. This is pressure. There is sweat.

10.30 AM: Head towards Limerick.

A Typical Day in the Early Years (Afternoon)

1 PM: Arrive back at the factory. I stopped for a twenty-minute snooze around 11 AM, followed by lunch at a lay-by outside Cork. Lunch – or perhaps more correctly, brunch – consisted of by-now-lukewarm coffee accompanied by some fruit, water and Carambola Kidz sandwiches. This, by the way is still my lunch today. (With the exception of the lukewarm coffee, as we now have a bean-to-cup machine in the office – Bewley's, naturally.)

Immediately upon my return, the real work starts. I pass the van over to one of the guys, who unloads it, cleans it and washes the trays for re-use. The Limerick route – at that stage outsourced to Noel Neville and Eddie Stewart, who are good people – is already completed, and those empties have been washed.

The sandwich-makers have been in since 8 AM, and there is always something that needs my attention. A supplier hasn't arrived yet, we got the wrong amount of something or other, one of the staff hasn't turned up but is on her way, there is a note to say a school rang to change Johnny's order or cheques need signing.

The tray-packers are also in. At this stage in our development, we have separated the various processes. We have a separate crew packing trays with everything other than sandwiches, which will be added later. All of the trays are labelled with the teacher, class and school and filled with water, juice, fruit and snacks. They are then placed in our cold room until we are ready to add the sandwiches.

There are suppliers to meet, samples to taste, production schedules to review, meetings to be had, brewing inter-depart-mental rows to head off. Stuff.

4 PM: It's late afternoon when the sandwich-makers finish production for the day and begin the 'clean down'. The tray-packers will continue for another few hours because they started later.

5 PM: As the last of the sandwich-makers leave, the sandwich-packers arrive. These are two guys who dress up like Eskimos and enter the cold room with class lists. They take one stack of trays at a time and, tray by tray, class by class, add the correct quantity of each sandwich type. Then they restack the trays in a fashion that allows them to be taken to the correct van the next morning in the correct order, so that the first tray in will be the last tray out at the last school on the van's route. They begin alone; I'll join them later.

7 PM: The tray-packing guys go home, leaving just me and the sandwich-packers in the building. I don my own Eskimo gear and head into the cold room, where the temperature is 5° Celsius – a full 10° Celsius warmer than the temperature outside when my day started fourteen and a half hours ago.

10.30 PM: Finished. Home to shower and bed for a few hours, assuming nobody has made a mistake. There is nothing worse at the end of an eighteen-hour day than finding you are missing three sandwiches when you get to the last tray. It's deeply frustrating to have to go back into the kitchen, gown up and make a handful of products because somebody messed up. Actually, there *is* something worse than being short by three sandwiches, and that is *being left with three sandwiches*! That means having to backtrack to find the mistake.

But Johnny must be fed. And he always was.

Collecting an Award

'Is that Colm O'Brien?' asked the unfamiliar voice on the other end of the line. 'Yes. Yes it is. Who's this?' I said into my Bluetooth earpiece, as I continued packing lunch trays. It was about 7 PM.

'Alan English, editor of the *Limerick Leader* newspaper,' he said. 'I'm calling to let you know you've been nominated as Limerick Person of the Month. Will you accept?'

'Say again?' I said incredulously. 'Who's this? What about an award? You're messin', right?'

I stopped packing the tray and moved to a place with better reception. He sniggered a bit as he replied.

'It's Alan English, editor of the *Limerick Leader*. We, along with some other sponsors, identify someone each month that is deserving of the award, Limerick Person of the Month. We think it should be you this month because of your good work with Limerick City Business Association. There will be a photo session this week and an awards ceremony at the end of the year, where all twelve Persons of the Month get presented and one will get chosen as Limerick Person of the Year. Would you like to accept?'

I was shaking my head and smiling broadly as I said, 'Of course. Thank you.'

He gave me some details and we hung up. I went back to packing lunch trays.

I've never worked for bonuses, and I've never done something just to get an award, but I find it very interesting that, if you do things right and for the right reasons, bonuses and awards happen.

I felt very honoured. Here was I, a Dub of all people – a

Leinster man in their midst – being singled out as deserving of being called Limerick Person of the Month. And for what? For doing something – that's the key here – for doing *something*. For not doing nothing. For not playing the victim in terms of my own Limerick city-centre business travails. In truth, for doing what just seemed like the right thing to do, not out of some sense of moral obligation, but out of a real sense of business desperation. And they wanted to give me an award for that? Well, I wasn't going to argue.

The day came. The line-up was announced, and it included an artist, a boxer, a grandmother, a developer, a diplomat . . . and a sandwich man.

Interestingly, I had been out of the city centre for some time, this being late 2006. The café had closed its doors over a year earlier. I had resigned as chairperson of the LCBA, passing the reins to the very capable Fionagh Ryan of a long-standing Limerick City institution, Ryan's Jewellers.

Fionagh joined Aido and I at the awards luncheon ceremony in the Clarion Hotel, the tallest hotel in Ireland, situated right on the beautiful Shannon River. The actor and celebrity Nigel Mercier was the master of ceremonies. Each Limerick Person of the Month was invited to the podium and presented with a beautiful, engraved piece of crystal.

When all twelve people were back in their seats, Nigel went on to announce the Limerick Person of the Year for 2005. And the winner was . . . not me.

Pat Cox, the former president of the European Parliament, a Limerick native, was justly awarded the honour.

Blow-up

My parents, Tommy and Doreen O'Brien, always told me, 'The man who never made a mistake, made nothing.'

I'm sure I heard that first after I had made a botch of something and needed comforting. To this day, I use those words to forgive myself for the many, many mistakes – some of which could have been avoided – I have made and continue to make as Carambola Kidz feeds Johnny.

One of my very early ones was promoting someone based on seniority.

We were growing at pace. Our system kept evolving. My dad, Tommy, had joined us in a sales role. He was sending us new business almost daily, as we opened up an entirely new market in the Irish school system. Carambola Kidz had cracked the nut and DEIS schools all over the country were clamouring for funding from the government, and looking for a reliable supplier. Carambola Kidz was it.

We were fast running out of space in Raheen, and everybody was being stretched way beyond what was comfortable for them. Most made the grade; some didn't. One individual who didn't – we'll call her Josephine – had joined Carambola Kidz early on. Since she was an early Carambola appointee and a hard worker, I relied on her more and more as new business came through the door.

New business meant more staff, more staff meant systems, training and supervision, and both Josephine and I assumed she would become the lead person in her area. It seemed natural and, from conversations with Josephine, it became very clear that anything else would have been unacceptable from her point of view.

She would be the first department head in our kitchen. Sorted. I was fine with that.

Anybody who knows me and has worked with me will testify to the fact that I love to see people wanting to get on, and am happy to facilitate opportunity. I particularly like growing the organisation from within, taking someone who has proven their worth and offering them first refusal on a new position, assuming they have the necessary talent, interest and qualifications. But, back in the early days, with such rapid growth and no real time or systems to test someone's talents, it was a case of 'all hands man the pumps' as we fed Johnny.

The cracks began to appear quickly once Josephine became the team leader. All of a sudden, it was 'her kitchen' and they were 'her staff' and she would run the kitchen the way she thought best, thank you very much, and my input was neither required nor welcomed. In certain circumstances this can be OK, I'm sure. Particularly if the subordinate has vastly more experience and greater credentials than the boss but, sadly, this was not the case. This, unfortunately, was the result of someone being promoted beyond their capability. My fault.

We were growing way too fast and needing to adjust and change our production plans sometimes in the middle of a production day. Her inexperience, coupled with her intransigence, proved to be a block in the system that needed to be removed. Mid-production one day, I called her into my office and told her how I needed the kitchen run, effective immediately. She blew up and walked out. That allowed a great person, Magda, to step up. Magda grew in Carambola to become head of purchasing.

Blowout

Business was ramping up. It looked like we would make it through, we would get Carambola Kidz to profit levels sufficient to allow us to begin to pay off our café debts and start to pay ourselves again.

I was still doing all the Cork deliveries myself, for two reasons: 1) this was the front face of the company, where our company interacted with the client daily, and I was unwilling at this early stage to trust Cork to anyone else; and 2) we couldn't afford a driver.

Everything was going swimmingly until one midwinter morning.

I was on my usual delivery route. I had to leave Raheen by a certain time to arrive in Cork by a certain time to make sure Johnny got fed on time. We couldn't afford to miss, or Johnny would go hungry. I was right on schedule.

It was still dark as I rounded a curve in the road at 7.45 AM, at the point where the Blarney road joins the N21. I was on time. Morning traffic was, as usual, getting heavy as I indicated right, to move into the outer lane to allow for seamless flow of traffic from the Blarney road. My speed was 100 kilometres per hour, the same as all the other cars, jeeps and vans.

Bang! I hit something. The van began to shudder violently as I struggled to keep control. I needed to get to the hard shoulder *fast*! I couldn't brake without causing a pile-up. So I began my move back across the inner lane, through the early morning traffic, through the extra traffic coming from Blarney, holding the van as steady as I could, swearing and praying out loud as I went.

When I finally made it, I found that I had hit something: the rim of the wheel had a six-inch 'V' in it, and the tyre was shredded.

It was then that I realised there was a line of vehicles in the hard shoulder. Another one came in after me. Nine cars, vans and jeeps had hit the same thing in the outer lane and all of them were damaged. That thing turned out to be a wheel. Someone, we found out later, had been transporting wheels in an open trailer. One had bounced out and come to rest in the fast lane. All the vehicles that hit it had suffered passenger-side blowouts. It was an absolute miracle that no one was injured or killed.

My problem was that I needed to feed Johnny. I had more than two thousand lunches in the back of the van, I had a schedule to keep and time was ticking away.

I made a flurry of phone calls, including one to the office to have someone there alert the schools that I would arrive later than usual but before *sos beag*. Soon, a recovery vehicle was on the way. A great guy came out in a suitably equipped truck. He raised my van, changed the wheel, left me the damaged one as a souvenir and helped me back on the road. I had lost a wheel and an hour.

I sweated more than ever as I raced around our client schools, delivering lunches with a fury. At 10.45, just before *sos beag*, I delivered the last load. I just about cried with relief. Before heading back to HQ, I slowly retraced my steps, school by school, and collected the empties, which I normally do when I make the deliveries.

As always, Johnny was fed.

Breakthrough

In 2004, a guy from Shannon Development had told me that the premises I wanted to view was too big for me. He was right at the time, but he couldn't see what I saw. Despite his protestations, we went ahead and rented the place anyway. One of my worst moments in that first premises occurred when I arrived one morning at 5 AM as usual to find the door smashed open. We had been burgled. I nearly vomited. All I could think was that we had thousands of mouths to feed all over the country in a few hours; I prayed the burglar hadn't touched the lunches.

I rang the gardaí and then entered the darkened building cautiously. The alarm was screaming, although it had been ripped from the wall. I couldn't silence it. My office door looked like a mallet had been taken to it; there was debris everywhere. I made my way to the cold room to find, to my tremendous relief, that nothing had been touched. Clearly our product was not of any value to the burglars.

The laptops were gone, as was some petty cash and my good camera. Doors, drawers and filing cabinets had been smashed, but they got nothing of real value. You see, the real value in our organisation is our product, our brand, our team and our shared ethos of feeding Johnny 100 percent on time, in full. That is where the real value lies in our organisation. The rest is just stuff, the rest is replaceable, but Carambola Kidz's reputation is not.

That morning the most important things – the lunches – were still there, thank God. Johnny was fed. Our reputation remained intact. Carambola Kidz got stronger.

We worked hard – very hard. We made mistakes. We had breakdowns and blowouts, break-ins and blow-ups. In June 2007, three years after we moved into Raheen, only two years after the café nearly took us under, we were able to buy and fit-out a brand-spanking-new premises, Carambola Kidz HQ, at Unit B5, Annacotty Business Park, Dublin Road, Limerick. That, my friends, was some moment.

The number of lunches we were delivering daily had grown from twenty-seven to seven thousand, with confirmed orders to bring us to thirteen thousand in September. We had clearly out-grown the 465 square metres available in Raheen, and so we moved, over the summer of 2007, to 1,300 square metres of bespoke kitchens and packing facilities, to allow us to cope with the increased business.

By January 2008, we had grown to twenty thousand lunches per day, which is where we are at still. Between then and now, we made more mistakes, took our eyes off the ball periodically and paid the price in terms of lost market share, all of which and more we have regained. (Perhaps that's all a story for another book.)

Throughout this tremendous journey, however, we have changed the landscape of school meals in Ireland forever. Our mission to promote healthy-lifestyle awareness in all children is being achieved in part because we forced all operators to raise their game. Children in disadvantaged areas in Ireland are being fed supremely well because of what Carambola Kidz has done.

We finally have breakthrough. Thank God.

CHAPTER 8
Ten Lessons I Am Learning as I Go

Lesson 1
Define the Big Picture
for *Your* Life

Whether you are considering going into business or you are already in business, it is important to remember that your business is not your life. It is probably a large part of it, and it deserves and requires its due commitment, but, really, if we are honest with ourselves, it is a means to an end. It is a creative outlet through which to express ourselves. It is a way to pay some bills and enjoy some comforts.

And it is for this very reason that I ask people attending my talks to do a particular exercise. They have to do it in public. You, the reader, get to do it in private – unless, of course, you are sitting in a café or on a train as you read this. It may feel a bit strange. It certainly looks strange. But it has proven to be a very powerful exercise for keeping things in perspective. So here goes.

1. Mentally add five years to your age and say the answer out loud. For some of us, this will be a wake-up call. We are no longer twenty-one. Time is getting shorter. This is the age you will be, please God, *regardless* of what you do in the next five years.

2. Get a mental picture of how you would like your life to look when you are that age, five years from now. Let me help here. Your business is cranking along beautifully, you are making some money, the bills are being paid, the kids are healthy, the car starts every morning and you have

your eye on a newer one, you are planning a nice family holiday in the sun, you and your other half having just come back from a skiing trip – all the stuff that will make your investment of time and effort over the next five years worthwhile. Now pick a prop in the room, perhaps a picture on a wall, a vase, a bottle or a chair – anything that is a few metres away – and imagine it is a mini video screen. Run the video of your life five years from now on your chosen video screen for a few minutes. Really get the feel of it. Enjoy the experience. This is what your life would look like if you waved a magic wand over it. When you have it clear, come back to step three. Take your time. This is your life.

3. Now reach out one arm in the direction of your video screen, stick up your thumb and close (or cover) one eye. If you are doing this correctly, you should be looking at the back of your thumb. Your video screen should be completely out of sight. Adjust your arm and thumb to achieve this. Once you are done, look at the back of your thumb for a minute, noticing how it has completely obliterated your view of your future life. When you are ready, proceed to step four.

4. Leave your arm and thumb in place in front of your future life so that you can visually toggle between it and this book. Your thumb represents a problem. Your plan was working swimmingly for three months, a year, even three years, perhaps. Now some big problem has come into your path as you work towards your future life: the kids are sick, the mortgage is in arrears, a supplier let you down, a staff member left and went into competition, a customer hasn't

paid, the banks are calling in their loan. The problem is *real* and *huge* and, as a result, deserves your full attention. So the plan for your future life gets put to one side while you handle it. And handle it you will! Do you know how I know you will handle it? Because 'they' – the famous committee of naysayers that plagues us all – said you would never make it. And you are not going to let them be right, are you? Dang right you're not. So you work doubly hard and, finally, you get past your problem. You can put your arm down now. Now what do you see in the distance, beyond where your thumb once was? In my talks, the relieved people in the audience usually put their arms down and, in unison, say 'our future life'. I imagine that's what's going through your head right now. Unfortunately, that's the wrong answer. What's looming in the distance, in front of your future life, is the next problem . . . the next thumb, getting larger by the day.

5. Arms and thumbs back up please. Block out your view of your future life again. Yes, you have hit another problem and, yet again, you are not going to let the committee of 'they' be right, so you redouble your efforts and knock down this thumb – and what's behind it? Yes, you're learning: the next thumb. And when you knock that one down, what will be behind it? Correct. The next thumb. The problem here is that, if we just focus on the problem and knock it down, only to find another one looming and then knock *it* down, knowing that there will be more coming after it, ad infinitum, we risk running out of steam. We risk becoming like those optimists who died of broken hearts in the POW camps. Life will just get too hard. We may decide 'they' were right all along, and throw in the towel

on our business. My theory is that this is why most new businesses fail in the first five years. The originators simply decide it's too hard, and give up. Now let me help you handle this reality. 'Phew,' I hear you sigh. Firstly, it's important we both agree that there will be problems in our lives in the next five years, no matter what. Whether you start a business or develop your existing one or not, there will be 'thumbs' in your life. They will simply be different types of thumbs if you are in business, that's all. Agreed? OK.

6. Arms out, thumbs up, one eye closed, future blocked, one last time. This time, leave your arm out and your thumb up, but open *both* eyes. Look at your future beyond the thumb. You can see your future clearly again, right? What has happened to the thumb? It's still there, isn't it? It's still real. It still has to be handled, but what has happened to its intensity? Am I right in saying it appears smaller, it's out of focus, you can see clearly beyond it? Can you see how, if you keep a clear eye on where you are headed – which is why you are in business in the first place – it will be easier to navigate around, over and under some thumbs that come your way? Or even avoid them altogether?

My dear, dear reader, I hope you took the time and allowed yourself the freedom to participate in this exercise. For me, it is fundamental. If you don't get a clear picture of why you are doing what you are doing, business *will* get too hard, the path of least resistance might be to throw in the towel and, if you do, the world will be poorer for it.

To paraphrase Admiral Jim Stockdale, 'Never lose faith that you will prevail in the end, whilst simultaneously confronting the most brutal facts of your current reality.'

Lesson 2
Time Management Doesn't Work

'I knew it!' I hear some of you cry victoriously.

Have I finally vindicated your way of being? Life is just too random to plan *anything*, so you have always simply chosen not to plan.

Regrettably, if that has been your reaction, I must burst your bubble. Planning is essential. But trying to manage time itself is impossible. Try stopping all the timepieces in your home or office for fifteen minutes and then restart them. What time is it? It's fifteen minutes later than your timepieces say it is. We can't manage time – it just keeps marching on.

So if you can't manage time, then what *can* you manage? The answer, which is at once both simple and complex, is *yourself*. You can manage what you *choose* to do at any and every given moment. That's it.

The late Stephen R. Covey, one of my all-time favourite motivational thinkers and trainers, in his book and CD series The Seven Habits of Highly Effective People, teaches us 'quadrant-two living' and his 'big rocks' theory. Within these concepts, he teaches us that we must first decide what is important in our lives, and then prioritise the activities that give us the desired results in these important areas. We must schedule time for these activities *first* each week, often by sacrificing less-important activities. As Stephen suggests, 'Organise and execute around priorities.'

Managing priorities works. Trying to manage time doesn't.

Lesson 3
Be Open to New Ideas

'You'd make a fortune if you had your own little coffee shop,' was the advice my dad used to give me. From his perspective, the advice was sound. But it was wrong for me. Thankfully, I resisted.

But because of my several decades of training in the café industry, opening coffee shops, not running my own little one, was the most obvious choice when I decided, in 2003, to attempt to 'build something significant'. At the time of writing, however, I am not in the coffee shop business. Over the years, my thinking has broadened, mainly as a result of reading books and listening to CDs to get other people's views of the world. I have become open to new ideas.

One of the great ideas I came across – and which I discussed earlier in this book – was the 'hedgehog' concept of business, from *Good to Great* by Jim Collins. This suggests that you ask yourself what you can be the best in the world at, and that it may *not* be what you are currently engaged in. I find this very liberating.

I believe that my business, Carambola Kidz, *is* the best in the world at feeding children in school. We are brilliant at it. We are on a mission to promote healthy-lifestyle awareness in all children. We have changed forever the way that children in disadvantaged schools in Ireland eat. Competitors in the industry set themselves up to be 'just like Carambola'.

Please be open to new ideas. The next one might spark something in you that will change the world. Imagine if I hadn't been open to new ideas.

Lesson 4
Network

Remember the man on the train? This entire story has been told because I met a man on a train. That was networking. It wasn't forced. There was no agenda, no 'you scratch my back, I'll scratch yours', but it *was* networking.

I was introduced to the term 'networking' through the business concept 'network marketing'. In the main, this is a sound way of doing business – buying from people you know, like and trust – but, regrettably, network marketing companies are often accused of teaching their members to see everybody as a suspect first, a prospect second and a member or a client third. They are people first, people second and still people, whether or not they become members or clients.

There are formal networking organisations, such as Business Network International, which teach people core skills around networking and espouse the motto 'givers gain', meaning that, if I help you get business, you will want to help get me business.

There are speed-networking events, where attendees are warned to bring *lots* of business cards. They are then encouraged to collect as many business cards as possible in five minutes or so. The net result of this type of activity is you walk away with fifty business cards belonging to strangers, most of whom you can't remember by the time you get home. They are consigned to the same drawer holding the hundreds of other strangers' business cards you have collected over the years. Have you ever bought from a stranger?

For me, networking is a profession, and I see myself as a professional networker. Not in a manipulative way, not in a formulaic way – simply in a human way. People make the world go round, not money; money is a tool and perhaps one type of reward.

Only this morning, I read a LinkedIn post by Sir Richard Branson. Referring to a column he read in the *Economist*, Sir Richard says:

> I was intrigued by Daniel Isenberg's interpretation; he believes "entrepreneurs are contrarian value creators. They see economic value where others see heaps of nothing. And they see business opportunities where others see only dead ends." Here, along with his opinion that policy makers need to remove barriers to entry for all sorts of businesses, I wholeheartedly agree.

> However, I completely disagree with his view that "the main motivator for entrepreneurs is the chance of making big money". If you get into entrepreneurship driven by profit, you are a lot more likely to fail. The entrepreneurs who succeed usually want to make a difference to people's lives, not just their own bank balances. The desire to change things for the better is the motivation for taking risks and pursuing seemingly impossible business ideas.

Somewhere along the line, I came across what I believe to be a truism: 85 percent of one's ability to succeed in any field relates to one's ability to work effectively with other people, and only 15 percent relates to technical ability.

My belief is that networking, like business, is not first about making money – it is about making a difference in people's lives. What worked about my meeting with the man on the train was the strapline on my business card, my offer to the universe, and the conversation it sparked. In an instant, we were no longer strangers.

Lesson 5
Be Flexible

Here's the thing. You've decided to start your own business, or perhaps go full-time in a venture that you once worked on in the evenings and on weekends, alongside your day job. Or perhaps you've simply decided finally to get stuck in and develop the thing you've been involved in for years, which has been bouncing along the bottom, never achieving enough momentum to break free and soar. And you're feeling good. But be warned. The ride ahead may not be as smooth as you hope. In fact, it is more likely that it will be very bumpy and appear to have a never-ending uphill trajectory.

This is normal. Expect it. Prepare for it. Plan for it.

You see, just because you finally decided to grab hold of your life and, as part of that, you made a commitment to build a business for yourself and your family, it doesn't mean the world will say, 'Finally! Best wishes,' and step aside to allow you to fulfil your dreams. On the contrary, while a whole host of unplanned and unforeseen events, people and resources will surely appear to help you on your way, there will also be a plethora of negative situations, roadblocks and even well-meaning loved ones who could knock you off course. Or perhaps, as I prefer to see things, to see what you are made of, to see if you are serious.

Let me deal with well-meaning loved ones first. It is important to understand that a) they really do love you and they want the best for you, and b) they really do mean well as they try to talk you down from your newly acquired lofty perch, with your fancy dreams. The problem is not your fancy dreams, but their paradigm, their unique way of viewing the world.

The very best way I have identified to ascertain whether advice from anyone – including well-meaning loved ones – is valid, is to ask myself which of Robert Kiyosaki's cash-flow quadrants it is coming from. If I want to build a business, but my cousin has been a government employee for twenty-five years, his opinion on my plan is *not* valid. It is impossible for him to have an accurate view of the world of business owners. If, however, Richard Branson, or some relative who has spent a life as a business owner, offered advice, I'd absolutely listen.

You have probably heard of the redwood trees of California. These truly are giants of nature. Some are more than 3,500 years old, a hundred metres tall and fifteen metres in diameter. To put this in perspective, Dublin's Spire monument is 121 metres tall and three metres in diameter. How have the redwoods survived for millennia and grown to such gigantic proportions, despite wind, rain, snow, storm and fire?

Part of the answer for their longevity and success resides in their relative flexibility. Trees are masters of going with the flow, and bending rather than breaking in the face of adversity. Another key factor is that they only grow in groves, never as standalones (*mé féiners* as we say in Ireland). They stand shoulder to shoulder with, dare I say it, like-minded trees – trees from the same quadrant. The smallest grove has six giant redwoods, and the largest has twenty thousand. Within these groves, the trees intertwine their massive roots, which gives them added solidity and assurance. They stick together and exude a 'whatever' attitude to the forces of nature, which exterminate the less flexible, less committed, more isolated wannabes.

My advice: learn to be flexible; bend, don't break; and be careful who you listen to as you build your business.

Lesson 6
Read and Study

I'm a Disney fan. When we went to Disney World in Florida for my fortieth birthday, it was our second visit. We have also been to the Californian and Parisian Disney parks several times each over the years. Everybody should go – they are absolutely wonderful – but don't forget to bring the kids! Anyway, most of what I want to talk about in this section is some advice from a Disney movie.

Who remembers *Pocahontas*? This was Disney's thirty-third animated movie, released in 1995. It was also the first Disney production based on a real historical figure: the Native American woman the film was named for. In the movie, Pocahontas meets and falls in love with a dapper English explorer, John Smith, who was also a real historical figure. Their real encounter didn't happen the way it was portrayed in the movie, but, as they say in Hollywood, 'Never let the facts get in the way of a good story.'

Picture this: Pocahontas is running through the forest, leading John Smith by the hand, showing him all the wonders of nature whilst challenging in song his – and the other settlers' – mindset. In the third verse of the movie's Oscar-winning song 'Colours of the Wind', she sings these powerful lyrics:

You think the only people who are people

Are the people who look and think like you

But if you walk the footsteps of a stranger

You'll learn things you never knew you never knew

Look at the fourth line again: 'You'll learn things you never knew you never knew.' My goodness that is powerful stuff! Not just things you never knew, but things you never even *knew* that you never knew. I love it!

You see, there is lots of stuff out there that we don't know, each of us, but there is *infinitely* more stuff out there that we don't even know that we don't know. So how *do* we get to stumble across stuff – concepts, ideas, facts – that we didn't know existed in the first place? One answer is to read books. Books represent someone else's view of the same world you and I inhabit and, if the author knows something that I never knew, she can impart it to me, I can learn from it and my world is instantly larger.

I was blessed. For me, apart from during my 'stupid phase' in my teens, reading has always been second nature, but I realise that not everybody has the same interest in books. I was doubly blessed when I was introduced to personal-development litera-ture on my twenty-first birthday through *Jonathon Livingston Seagull*. But it was getting into the habit of reading a personal-development or business-related book for ten minutes every day, and then studying biographies and autobiographies of world leaders, that really began to shape the world I now inhabit.

This might have been lesson number one – it is that impor-tant. The reason I decided not to put it first is that you won't change your reading habits unless you have a reason to, so get-ting the big picture of your life has to come first. You should approach all your reading the same way that I suggested, in the introduction, that you approach reading this book: discipline yourself to read either ten minutes or ten pages a day. Do this every day for the next year, with books that stretch your mind. Afterwards, if your life is not measurably fuller, bigger, more exciting and more flush with possibilities, I'll buy from you – at face value – the twelve personal-development or business-devel-opment books you have read. Guaranteed.

Lesson 7
Get Good People on Your Team

'Colm, I've looked at the problem and I have three possible ways to resolve it. Option A has this catch, Option B allows us this amount of flexibility, Option C is a just-in-case job. My recommendation is that we go with Option A. If you agree, sign here.'

This is how Brian Meehan, my friend and Carambola Kidz's finance director, deals with me. He is a detail fanatic, it is fair to say. I am not. Brian's strengths offset my weaknesses and vice versa. That's what makes us a good team.

Recently, Aido and I had the pleasure of seeing our son, Steven, along with a cast of thirty, wow the audience at the new, state-of-the-art Lime Tree Theatre in Mary Immaculate College, Limerick, with a performance of *Cats*, the musical. It was, as one punter put it, a production worthy of the West End, truly mesmerising.

We attended on the final night, the night when plaudits and flowers are showered on all and sundry. The cast came out for their curtain call and, as is the norm in a show of this kind, the support characters and chorus lines came first, followed in ascending order by the people playing the plot's more involved characters, the applause getting louder the more important the character was to the plot. You know the score: predictable, but well deserved.

What was equally impressive, however, was that the behind-the-scenes crew members were called on stage to be honoured for their parts in the production. Several things struck me that night as I watched dozens more people – set designers, choreographers, lighting and sound assistants, musicians, make-up artists and poster hanger-uppers – shuffle on in groups, completely uncomfortable in the limelight, to well-deserved applause.

First, it struck me that without these backstage people the show could not have gone on. The cast on stage needed the backstage crew and the backstage crew needed the cast on stage; neither group could have comfortably done the work of the other. Second, everybody had obviously volunteered according to his or her personally perceived strengths. Third, it all needed managing – thus the position of director, capably filled by Sadhbh Nic Aodha – and overseeing, an equally unenviable task, undertaken by Dr Mike Finneran, head of the college's Department of Arts Education and Physical Education.

The parallels between all of this and any business on the planet were not lost on me that night. Every business, if it is to grow, needs a team of people with complementary – not competing – talents. The front-line or front-of-house people can only be effective in their roles if the background or back-of-house people are capably producing; the back-of-house people are relying on the front-of-house team to provide them with meaningful work to do.

'But I'm a one-man band,' you say. No you're not. You need a bank manager, don't you? She's on your team. Supplier? He's on your team. Telephone and Internet provider? Part of your team. Have you a spouse? On your team. Kids? Your team. Mechanic to keep your car or van on the road? Team. You may be the only person being officially paid (or, in most start-ups, not being paid) by your venture at present. You may be the overseer, manager, producer and even the product at this stage in your business's development, but none of us works in isolation.

The word 'TEAM' can be seen as an acronym standing for 'together, everybody achieves more'. Make sure the people you attract complement your strengths and, when you find the ones who you would trust your family with, keep them.

Lesson 8
Deal with Issues

In his book *Losing My Virginity*, Sir Richard Branson tells of a business-class passenger on Virgin Atlantic who had encountered a problem. Her electronic wheelchair had been broken during a flight, and it had caused her significant stress, not to mention inconvenience. She was furious, and told the staff in no uncertain terms that she would never fly Virgin again; she was taking her business to British Airways, Virgin's nemesis.

Word got back to Richard. What did he do? He rang her, that's what he did. Sir Richard Branson, the knighted multi-billionaire founder of the Virgin Group, picked up the phone and called this woman at her home one night and, after he had introduced himself (can you imagine?), apologised and told her that he understood her position. Even though she may never fly Virgin again, he said, there was a motorcycle courier en route to her home as they spoke with a catalogue of specialist electronic wheelchairs. He asked her to pick one and promised it would be delivered to her in the coming days, courtesy of Virgin Atlantic.

That, my friends, is dealing with an issue.

Now, lest we start thinking think the only issues we have to deal with are our customers' issues, nothing could be further from the truth. Every interaction, every relationship in the team we spoke of earlier, has the potential to cause an issue. You may have spousal issues to handle, banker issues to take care of, supplier challenges, cash-flow problems, staff personality spats, product deficiencies, lawsuits, insurance claims or offspring problems. It could be anything.

An unresolved issue is like a cancerous cell in a body. Untreated, all issues are detrimental to the development of your business, and some can be fatal.

Tommy O'Brien, my dad, has always said that when there is a problem, the relationship can only go one of two ways: it can either improve or 'dis-improve', but it can *never* be the same. Experience has taught me that he is right. Someone once said, 'It's not what happens, but how we *deal* with what happens that's important'.

The truly wonderful thing about problems – and perhaps their universal function – is that they point very specifically to something we can and must fix. Back in my early café days with Stephen Halpin at Clerys and Hallins, we used comment cards on the tables. You know the type of thing: a card inviting you to tell us how we did during your visit, in relation to food quality and temperature, customer service, speed of service and cleanliness of facilities. Most were glowing, which, while lovely to hear, was frankly a waste of good trees. The ones that had value, that held the nuggets of gold, were the ones that said, 'Today you sucked at . . .' Because those ones gave us chances to review the issues and take appropriate corrective action.

A word of caution here: you have to learn to understand the difference between one-off problems, which may be more to do with the person complaining, and real problems that need your time and attention. Try, if possible, to avoid knee-jerk responses to one-offs. When possible, bide your time, cultivate patience and look for a pattern. If the problem raises its head again and again, it is real; if it doesn't, it may not be. That said, don't – on pain of death – act like an ostrich when it comes to issues. Do not put your head in the sand and hope they will go away all on their own. Not only will they not go away, the sand can act like fertiliser – they will often grow!

Lesson 9
Choose to Never Lose

Sounds good doesn't it? Never experiencing a loss again?

Clearly it can't happen and, even if it could, it wouldn't be healthy. But it is your choice how you interpret it when you don't win in life.

Sometime, something you try will not work, guaranteed. Perhaps, before reading this book, you would have considered that losing, but, if you've been attentively following my journey, you will have come across Chapter 5, in which we discussed shifting the way we look at these situations, from 'losing' to 'learning'.

Regrettably, success teaches us nothing. Remember the comment cards in the café? Hearing over and over again that you are great, that everything is wonderful, can lead to complacency. It is only when we underperform at something, and we interpret that as a loss that we might consider making changes. If we do, we regain our power over the perceived loss, converting it into a lesson – we move from 'losing' to 'learning'.

In business, I hope you experience loss sooner rather than later. This is not me wishing failure on you. It is simply me hoping that you experience not winning early on, so that you will learn two things quickly: first, how to win again the next time the same situation arises; and second, more importantly, that you are capable, that you have fortitude – that you're a survivor.

I'm reminded of another movie, which I expect most of you may be familiar with: *Home Alone*, starring Macaulay Culkin as an eight-year-old boy who is accidentally left behind while his family flies to France for Christmas and has to defend his home against idiotic burglars, one of whom is played by Joe Pesci. For me, this movie was completely laugh-out-loud funny. The comedic pain inflicted on the two burglars was palpable. I felt for them as I laughed uncontrollably at their misfortune.

There is, however, some mild threat implied in the plot and, at one point, Culkin is scared stiff. After all, he is only eight and he realises that his home is under attack. He panics and hides under the covers of his parents' bed, hoping they will return and the burglars will disappear. A seminal moment occurs when he realises that this is not going to happen, that he is the man of the house and, if it is going to be defended, he must do it alone.

Once he has this realisation, he literally starts jumping up and down on the bed – the same one he had been hiding in – shouting, 'I'm not afraid anymore! I'm not afraid anymore!' The situation hasn't changed. Yet. He is still alone. But he has *decided* not to be scared. He has *decided* to do something about it.

This, my friends, is what I'm wishing for you: that moment when you have not won something, when your worst fear has come to pass, when you are hoping your mother will come in and kiss it all better and sort it all out so you don't have to and when you finally realise that that's not going to happen and say to yourself, 'If it is going to be, it's up to me. I'm not afraid anymore. I'm not afraid anymore!'

At that moment, you will know the full meaning of 'sometimes I win, and sometimes I learn.'

Lesson 10
Be Thankful and Believe

I'm not grateful enough for all the good stuff in my life. I am healthy, I have meaningful work to do, my family are still with me, the bills manage to get paid, I was born to great parents, I'm Irish . . . the list could go on and on. The point is, I find it easier to focus on the one or two areas that aren't what I wish they were. Do you know anybody like this? I bet you do.

My recommendation to you is that you consider taking stock of the good things in your life more often, to remind yourself that the good stuff outweighs the bad stuff, probably by a factor of several times. Stephen R. Covey, in his lessons, talks about the week being the perfect 'patch' in the fabric of life: there are work-days, mornings, evenings and the weekend – and then it starts again. I like thinking that life is made up patches, each one only week long. It makes for great planning, and is ideal for a review of the type I am talking about. I typically use Sundays to have a look at what shape my life is in – not in a morbid, introspective way, just in the sense that I take a cursory glance at it to see if I am on track. Think about it.

Finally, there are three things I recommend you consider believing in, the first of which is God. Now, I realise we all inter-pret the world differently, and I am not trying to preach, but I must share what works for me. I was baptised Catholic shortly after birth, as was the tradition for the majority in Ireland for many years. I had no choice in the matter. As the years went on, I made my own choice to continue in that belief system. I believe

Colm O'Brien

I am a child of God and that Jesus came to earth to remind us of that fact and, in conquering death on the cross, he conquered the final frontier – there is nothing to be afraid of.

I make God real in my life. I turn up believing I am playing a part in His plan, not mine. This book is part of it. I have no idea where it will lead, but He does. By the way, I take God into meetings with me and ask Him to sit in a chair, ideally next to me. I will regularly lean over and pat the chair to help me regain my composure if I feel the need. I have to admit that there have been several times in difficult meetings where I have asked Him to zap my adversary; to date, no joy . . . but I live in hope.

Second, I recommend you believe in the inherent goodness of most people. Most people are willing to help if asked. There are shysters out there for sure, but they are tragic people whose self-worth is derived from hurting others. They exist, but they are few and far between. Let's not allow them and their behaviour to stop us from being open, loving and trusting, in the belief that the majority are like you and me: out there trying their best with the best of intentions.

Last, and we finish here ladies and gentlemen, I recommend you believe in yourself. There is nobody on the planet sitting in your seat as you read these words but you. Nobody with your unique set of skills and life experiences looking at the world in quite the way you do, but you. Nobody can do what you can in the unique way that you can but you. Why can't the next Google, Starbucks, Guggenheim, Eiffel Tower – the next world-changing idea – come from you? No reason. Except, perhaps, that you don't believe it can. If you don't do what's in your heart to do, I believe the world will be a poorer place.

Thanks for thinking with me through these pages. Let's go make a difference.